IN THE
SHADOW OF
WRATH

IN THE SHADOW OF WRATH

A Veteran's Journey

JERRY MITCHELL

IN THE SHADOW OF WRATH

iUniverse books may be ordered through booksellers or by contacting:

iUniverse
1663 Liberty Drive
Bloomington, IN 47403
www.iuniverse.com
1-800-Authors (1-800-288-4677)

ISBN: 978-1-4917-5606-5 (sc)
ISBN: 978-1-4917-6458-9 (e)

Library of Congress Control Number: 2015902339

Print information available on the last page.

iUniverse rev. date: 03/30/2015

To MY LOVING parents, Fred (Bud) and Sally Mitchell, who sacrificed much for the children and gave up everything to escape the wrath. The difficult decisions they made literally changed the lives of the family. It caused a disconnection between the family ties of those left behind and the family that migrated, these ties were never restored. Each child had to learn and appreciate what little he or she had. The strengths derived from the decision, the changes, and the experiences in my life were huge.

Acknowledgments

I want to thank my buddy and writer Jai Farris-Colvin for writing and reviewing the foreword and introduction and also for encouraging me.

A special thank-you to my lovely wife, who has been very patient and understanding and has been a great supporter in my efforts, putting her pains and illnesses aside.

Also a very special thank-you to my Navajo Indian and Vietnam combat buddy, Richard "Kee" Yazzie, for using his artistic creativity. He was able to view my sketch and idea and draw the cover for my book.

Most of all, I thank and give praise to the Lord, our creator, for giving me the inspiration and words to share with others the journey, changes, and decisions made and the paths followed in order to trust and utilize my given talents.

I also want to thank my good friends Arnold and Irene Gomez (Fresno) for their efforts, concern, and help in getting the work done.

Foreword

There are many reasons to write a book. Some write books to remind themselves not to make the same mistakes. Others write them to pass on history. Some people write books in an attempt to understand themselves or the world around them. The author is writing this book for a collection of these reasons and more. He is writing because he has to; by the end, the reasons are clear. It seems there always comes a time in a man's life when he feels compelled to tell his story.

These stories are what he remembers. His life has risen and fallen as the ocean's tides, and he is proud to say that because of the strengths of those who came before him, he has weathered well. He recalls stories told by his elders that pushed him toward the life he was to lead. Many times they pointed him in the right direction or would be soothing in the rough times. A strong will and a marked desire to get things done have been handed down through the years from his great-grandparents, his grandparents, and his mother and father. Perhaps after reading this book, readers will gain a better sense of their own families and the history that makes them who they are. We as humans don't just pop into existence—our lives are a series of events propelled through time by those who come before us and those who will come after us. The history of a family is entwined within its members, and for most, that history begins with a family name.

As we age, our curiosity about who we are and where we came from intensifies, and we find ourselves asking questions like, where did our family name originate, and how has it evolved through the decades? Where we were from, and what brought our particular family to where we are now? Many are surprised to discover the answers to these questions, and some even discover that their families have had an impact on so much more than they ever could have imagined.

History shows us that we are affected by those who have gone before us. The author has personally often wondered how his life would be different if the paths of his parents, grandparents, and great-grandparents had been different. What if they had chosen a different fork in the road? What kind of man would he be today?

We as individuals are a direct product of circumstances in our history. We would not be "us" if our parents had married a different person. If our grandparents had moved to a different part of the country, if great-grandparents had settled in Canada instead of the United States, we would each be a different person … With one broad stroke of a different pen, our paths could have been drastically different. The author often wonders who he would be. How would he have acted differently? Would his values and ideals be different? In his mind, history is so important to who we are as individuals that the slightest change in the course of our lives can mean a totally different outcome.

Perhaps this is what truly makes us who we are; we are the sum of our experiences, good or bad. History is a part of the balance in our lives that makes it possible for us to be who we need to be in order to answer the very call of what our souls are meant to accomplish in the few short decades that we are here on planet earth. Much of the author's own history is deeply embedded in one particular experience that he hopes to pass along within in this book.

As a veteran of the Vietnam conflict, he carries with him today the scars of what was through the memories of lives lost, battles won, and eventually a return home to a world so changed that many of the soldiers who were involved in the war hardly recognized it or themselves when they came home. His hope in telling his stories of that particular time in his life is that others who have family members who have also experienced war might better understand what their loved ones have gone through.

While writing this book, he came to realize how much of who he is was wrapped up in this youthful experience of being tasked with the responsibilities of men perhaps even before he was ready for it. So many of the younger generations today have no concept of the effects the war had on the generation who came before them. And today there are others coming home from fighting other wars who also have lived the experiences of the monumental task of protecting the country. These men and women have also come home with the scars of war. Hopefully, this book will also help their families understand them just a little better as well.

Although each soldier has individual experiences during his or her tour, there are also collective experiences that every veteran shares. This, the author hopes to share with you here. For those who went to fight in Vietnam, many weren't ready. They went from having an ideal life in the comfort of their homes to the chaos that is war. The author didn't have the benefit of this level of security. He joined the military after completing two years of college in an effort to make his own way in life. Once he finished his military basic training, the decisions made by his parents had clearly become his own.

When year eighteen hits, most of those same children will go off to a good college so they can obtain a good job and then continue the circle that is life with the creation of their own families. There is, however, a second group of children. These kids have lived a rougher path without the benefit of all that planning in their lives. For these kids, college is not an option. So instead, they join the ranks of the military in an effort to fill in the space left to them by parents who might also have not had the advantages of privileged kids. They too will gain experience like those in college; however, that experience will be very different.

At eighteen years old, when a person is supposed to be spreading his wings and stepping off into all that life has to offer, this group of kids instead is given a healthy dose of reality. They travel from the comfort of their homes to the actuality of what it means to be handed the responsibility of defending the rights of their fellow citizens. The cost of being a free nation is one that this group of kids is intimately aware of, because they will pay the cost with their very innocence.

The author was one of those kids. Right out of high school, the military is a shock to the average person. The lessons learned are far removed from adding and subtracting, geography and science. The lessons of the military are foreign at first. Learning to fight, handle a weapon, and survive. Although every new recruit goes through the same training, it affects each and every one of them differently, depending on their life experience thus far.

In basic training, the drill sergeants take a person's physical, mental, and spiritual strengths and tear them right down to the core. Long gone are the days of running to Mom and Dad; here at basic, you will be rebuilt. During training, the new soldiers are broken down until all that came with them from home is torn from their very souls. The soldier is then reprogrammed to handle the deadliest of weapons, live in the moment, and apply himself to the very core beliefs of the military, which may mean the difference between life and death once the soldier is on the battlefield.

Once the training was done for the author, He learned that he would be deployed to either an area of peace or one of conflict. The conflicts the United States usually gets involved with are ones in which another country has asked for our help. While deployed, the newly minted soldier begins the long arduous task of reinventing his or her family.

Long gone are the little brothers and sisters of yesterday. In their place is a group of people who have each been reinvented. A soldier begins to bond with the people within his squad and platoon. He begins to build a sense of trust that he will take with him everywhere he goes. These are ties that will bind a person for the rest of his life, and somehow, in the beginning, he senses this. There are many kinds of soldiers in a war. Some come to pull their duty and go home. These folks are only interested in serving their time.

Then there are the ones who don't know how to come home—the ones who become so connected to the fighting and surviving that they reenlist time and time again. These guys are so connected to the idea of standing for something greater than themselves that they learn to live within the conflict. To insinuate that the soldiers who are left behind when their tours end will somehow suffer is a driving force for some soldiers to reenlist. These guys sign on the dotted line once more, unable to stop protecting those with whom they have bonded. These guys want a "normal" life with a home and kids and a wife, but somehow, due to their time serving, the concept of "normal" eludes them.

When they do finally make that leap back into society, they discover that it's more difficult than they could have imagined. Many of these soldiers come back to a world that they never quite feel like they belong to. War has affected them forever. There are many words that get thrown around when a soldier returns from war. Post-traumatic stress disorder has now replaced words like *damaged, inconsolable, angry,* and *depressed.* Some carry home with them physical scars, some emotional ones, and some carry both. But no matter what the damage looks like, the damage is there, and these soldiers are forever changed.

Their "readjustment" back into the mainstream is painful at best and debilitating at worst. The life they once knew before the war is forever changed. These soldiers of freedom find themselves like fish out of water with no water in sight. Many family members who receive their loved ones back from a war have a tough time understanding what has happened to these guys and girls that they have sent off to war. They have a tough time relating to these strangers who are now standing in their living rooms, especially those involved directly in fighting. These once young kids return weathered and worn by war. They see the world through different, more pessimistic eyes. They have seen the world they wouldn't wish on their worst enemy.

Hopefully, you have received a sense of what it was like for these young kids. It is important that a person understands how the soldier lived and how he survived and, more importantly, how he returned. You are going to need this understanding to hear his story.

When he returned from his tour of duty in the infantry

after serving his time in the Republic of Vietnam, the author was different. He was changed. He was also damaged. And to make matters worse, soldiers returned from the war they didn't start or ask to fight in. They were spit on, snarled at, glared at, and called baby killers. By the time they returned from the Vietnam conflict, the popular opinions of the bulk of the citizens of the United States was that we were somehow a part of the problem. Our loyal service to our nation in the name of freedom became something to be despised. Many of them didn't understand then nor now, almost forty years later. It can honestly be said that in some ways, many still don't understand.

On one level, many do get it. Most people watched the news and believed what the media told them. Some couldn't stand the idea that fellow citizens were capable of killing others in the name of anything. Most households were removed from the real fighting of World War I and II because television didn't bring it into their living rooms. The Vietnam conflict was different. It was up close and personal, as well as being brutal. Most of the veterans from the Vietnam conflict still struggle to recover today. They live with PTSD (post-traumatic stress disorder), which consists of a bevy of side effects from their time in service.

Today, the author still struggles, although quietly and with more reserve. He can only imagine that for many of the others, the Vietnam conflict continues. Only now it is a struggle within.

Introduction

Have you ever watched a grandparent, uncle, or aunt thumb through old photos? They seem to somehow place an importance on those photos that, *unless* you understand the story behind the picture, you likely won't get. They treasure those memories. Just like that old, worn family Bible or that small garden patch that your mom put in when you were little. It still yields a few tomatoes. Those photos are part of the foundation that makes us who we are. Holidays spent with older family members can be eye-opening or a learning journey into the family history. Older generations have something the younger ones don't yet. They have history tradition.

These folks understand the importance of our past and what it means to preserve it for future generations. For most people, the way they learn about their history is through older relatives. Elders recite stories about traditions and culture to those generations who will follow them. For most of the history of man, this is how we as a species have survived, by passing on our history to our young so that they might learn from our mistakes and correct their own paths accordingly. Within each branch of man, from family to extended family, to the human race as a whole, our history is often complicated and extensive. Without the verbal history being passed down from generation to generation, mankind might cease to exist

It is with this in mind that I now convey my story, my history if you will. I have a long and involved history that includes both English and Irish traditions sprinkled with a bit of Dutch on my father's side of the family.

On my mother's side, I have roots in the Native American tribes of the nations. A great-great-grandfather who served as a Chickasaw chief gives me a deep sense of connection to the land that I was born in. I would not know of these beginnings if I hadn't had my family elders to pass along this information to me. I know other people who have no idea where they are from, and I have to say that I feel blessed that I do.

It is with this deep sense of history that I am able to add to my own story in the pages that follow. Heritage and roots are the solid bases from which I tell my stories, tracing my traditions and culture to times before I was born or even my father was born. I have used a great many resources while researching my family history.

Written and oral records are joined with church rolls, property ownership records, and even court records in the writing of this book. Along the way, I have uncovered many interesting stories about my ancestors that have helped me to understand some of my own personal history. I have listened to my elders tell their stories, and in doing so, I began to build a living family tree.

That family tree is long from finished growing. I, as well as those who will come after me, will continue to add to that tree, and it will forever grow toward new heights with each new generation. I'd like to encourage those who may have picked up this book to also consider tracing their heritage. There can be great joy in exploring the past through old family Bibles, stories of the past, and even scrapbooks.

Following your own story into the past may answer

important questions about health issues or personality traits. It is intriguing to follow the story into days gone by, and once you begin, you just never know where that story might take you. So now we begin my story—one of strife, struggle, and eventually survival of a simple family made up of the sum parts of the cultural melting pot that is America.

I will guide you through the struggles of my parents as they attempted to find their place in the world through the tough times of early America when the land was as young as the people who were trying to tame it. And finally, I will lead you into my story. I believe that by the end of this series of writings, you will see the clear connection between my family's past and my own present.

In chapter one of this book, I mention John Steinbeck's *The Grapes of Wrath*. This story is and always has been very important to me because my family lived through the times Steinbeck describes in his story.

My parents and my four older sisters lived the dust bowl years and survived to share their stories. Through the eyes of my sisters, I saw the after effects of the dust bowl years—like the way they saw food, for example. Having to go hungry gave them all an appreciation for hard work and a good meal that many folks today could never understand. Through my family, to some degree, I survived the dust bowl years too. My story now begins with the difficult life of a sharecropper in the 1920s.

My parents had eight children in the shadows of the wrath, which is where I was born. My parents were a small part of the larger migration that took place. However, the dust bowl was a large part of what shaped their lives and the lives of their children. It is where my story actually begins … in Oklahoma … in the dust bowl days … on the path to a new world.

Chapter 1

Dust Bowl Days

The dust bowl days in America were a period of the worst of times for Americans and their families. The first of the worst times was in 1929 when the stock market collapsed, and Americans lost everything they had (both finances and property). After struggling and rebuilding their lives and families, America also experienced the worst drought in our history, which smothered America's heartland, destroyed crops, and burned the soil. Giant walls of dust rolled across the soil, taking much of the dirt into the air and moving one farmland to another, tearing down structures and fences and killing livestock.

The Grapes of Wrath, written by John Steinbeck in 1939, was based on the dust bowl of America and the days that followed. On one level, it is a story of a family's struggle for survival in the Promised Land. On another level, it is a story of a people's struggle—"the migrants." It is also a story of America and the retelling of the biblical story of the Israelites and their exit out of Egypt. It becomes the story of mankind's quest for profound comprehension and of his commitment to his fellow man and to the earth he inhabits.

My parents and three older sisters were directly affected by this time in America's history that caused the largest migration of hardworking Americans from the heart of America's food-producing regions to the western regions of Arizona and California.

It was this migration and my family's history prior to it that I will focus on and share my research. I mentioned the importance of knowing and understanding the origin and heritage of one's family history. Knowing can come from talking to and listening to the stories as they are told by elder members of the family, including uncles, aunts, grandparents, and even Mom and Dad. The other technique of knowing about one's family tree is the through the use modern-day research methods, namely the computer to log on to Ancestry. com or various other websites to gather information and grow your own family tree.

Of the many branches my on family tree, I will attempt to explain the growth of the one branch I am most familiar with. One fork of the branch starts with my dad's parents, Tude Mitchell and Rosie Watts. From information I can compile, Tude met and married Rosie in the late 1890s in the Oklahoma Territory. Tude was a sharecropper (farmer), and lovely Rose was a housewife who cared for the four boys and one girl, as well as doing the cooking and cleaning for the small house.

Because they lived in the late 1800s and early 1900s, there is not much known about their life except that they were hard workers and reared five children (probably brats). The youngest of the five was my father, Fred Elmer, who was born June 5, 1901. He must have been a hard worker but found the time to meet and court Sally Jane Gaddis. (More info on Sally to follow.)

The story I was told many times was that Fred E. would remove his clothes down to his undies. He placed his clothes on a makeshift raft he'd made and would swim across the small river to visit Sally. Sally would anxiously wait for him, because she would have a picnic basket. They would go to their spot on the riverbank and enjoy the lunch. Many times, Fred would help her cook the evening meal for her family. Their courtship began and eventually led to the lighting of a bright flame, which lasted a lifetime. The two were married in a small garden setting in about 1925. The happy couple worked hard together to make a good life for themselves.

But something happened to interrupt their good life plans when on October 15, 1928, a surprise plump of a joy was delivered to them. Their first child was born—Betty June. The birth occurred in a neighbor's house a ways down the road. The neighbor had multiple experiences with birthing children, so she wanted to help the young couple out. The happy couple took the young'un and went back to their little place they called home.

As Betty June continued to grow, Fred and Sally continued working at whatever work they could get. Early one day in July 1929, Sally couldn't go to work to help Fred out because she was not feeling well. It must have been a touch of the flu with all the wind and dust blowing around.

The weather conditions adversely affected any work being done on the farm where Fred worked. Bewildered and confused, they kept working beside each other. Fred must have noticed that Sally appeared to be eating well, because she began putting on a little weight, but they kept on keeping on. As time passed, they noticed Sally was putting on more weight each month. But on March 3, 1930, they found out why she had put on the extra weight. Sally gave birth to the happy couple's second daughter, who they named Virginia Lee.

Now Virginia was a joyous welcome to the small family. Even "big sister" Betty June helped out as much as she could. A person knows that a two-year-old can be a lot of help around the small house with the chores as a big sister.

Well, the happy couple continued working hard, but now Sally had to stay home more to care for the two chunky bundles, who needed lots of care. Fred kept working hard at whatever work he could get. When the Great Depression began in 1929, work became scarce, and life for Fred and Sally became more difficult. However, the family production continued.

When the month of June came around, they got ready for the third stork to fly over. They waited and waited. Finally on June 15, 1931, a third daughter arrived, and they named her Colleen. Now what in the world were they going to do with three? Somehow, Fred managed to find enough work to sustain the growing girls and Sally.

I am sure that Fred was not real sure what happened in March 1931, but once again, Sally got to feeling a little faint. Was it the flu again? Well, on December 10, 1934, I bet you can guess what happened. It wasn't the rain or an improvement in the economy. A fourth daughter was born to the happy couple. I doubt if the three older sisters of Delois Jean were too excited about having another baby in the small, weathered house; after all, she was the baby girl now.

With the family getting bigger (literally) and work in Oklahoma getting harder to find, Fred had to make a decision. After hearing a few friends talking about all the work going on in Arizona and getting them to help load some of their belongings and essential household items, Fred made an important decision to follow the tracts of the neighbors and travel to Arizona. I am very sure that Sally was not to excited with the idea of packing up some of their stuff (as many had done weeks and month before) and moving her girls to some place where she had never been, never seen, and did not know where it was. Sally must have agonized over which items to take with them and which ones to leave. The space was limited; family members were going to be left behind also. Her heart must have been hurting.

But being the obedient good wife she was, she and Fred

packed what they could load into their vehicle and box trailer and headed out west. They later jokingly claimed that they almost did not have room for the girls.

It seems that my family members made a stop for about nine or ten years in Cold Water, Arizona. Since Arizona's temperatures do not get cold too often, the name of the town was later changed to Avondale. It is not where Avon products come from. Avondale is located just south of Interstate 10, east of Phoenix about twenty-five or so miles.

One of the early stories I heard about the vehicle (thought to be a 1932 or 1934 Plymouth sedan) that my parents used to leave the disastrous situation of the dust bowl was that he went to a small dealership to take a test drive. They later joked that the test drive ended when the trip to Arizona ended. Years later, I learned that dad had purchased the vehicle from a local resident who was also leaving the effects of the dry dirt and wind-blowing dust.

In the days of this great migration, there was no such things as ice chests to keep drinks cool and fresh as there is today. These drifters did the only thing they could to keep their traveling water cool. They hung their filled water bags on the bumper guards of their cars. They usually loaded a mattress or two on top, tied them down, and down the road they went in search of paradise and a better life. Upon arriving in Arizona, there was work waiting for them.

It was as if they had been told "plant the lettuce, and they will come." Life was still hard for the drifters. The severe heat and dryness of the Arizona desert made working in the lettuce and vegetable fields difficult, but the three most exciting events occurred during their stay.

The first was that Mom "got the flu" again. However, she had three older girls to help her get better. Lois, the youngest, was about two years old and didn't know anything about her getting sick. There was a little weight gain, which made it obvious that the flu was out of the question again. So during the scorching heat of the Arizona desert, my mom gave birth to my parents' first (count them) son, who was presented to Dad.

The newborn became Dad's namesake and was named Fred (middle name of Allen). Now, events can be peculiar when a baby is just born and on the way home to meet its siblings. With my parents being nervous, the blanket that was used to shield him from the elements slipped off of about half of his small and tender body, exposing it to the sun's UV rays and causing that half to slightly burn. The story that I have heard for years was that the blanket slipping and the sun's rays burned the delicate baby skin. As a result, he now has one blue eye and one brown eye and only sweats and has body hair on one side of his body. This is true. However, the cause is believed to be a medical condition, which is not serious.

The second exciting event came to pass after the flu symptoms again, which resulted in another birth—the last of five girls to be born to this hard-working couple from Oklahoma. However, the last of the five did not wait for the entire nine months to pass. She was anxious to meet her four sisters and her baby brother who was swimming through the terrible twos and wanted out about the seventh month. Along with this desire of baby Carol, came some birth difficulties. Not only should she have been ready two months early, but the desire to be born too early caused the placenta to come out before her. As a result of this, Mom lost so much blood that she could have died. During the difficult time, my mom was taken care of by neighbors and the older girls. The doctor did play a big part in her recovery.

Chapter 2

My birth, which was the most exciting event that occurred in Arizona, happened four years after the premature birth of the fifth and last girl. Due to the importance of this event, you will have to pay very close attention. Mom's flu symptoms occurred again about four years later, but this flu was not like the other six she had experienced. Once my mom began to gain a little weight, it wouldn't stop. As the months passed by, bigger and bigger she became. I don't recall, but about six or seven months into the pregnancy, I was told, my mom began having to wear stomach-support apparatus called a maternity corset that supported her big stomach and had straps that went over her shoulders. After about two months fighting with the support apparatus, she very happily gave birth to a second son. This son, she named Jerry. As an adult, it was apparent that I became more attached to family and helping out others. I did help my parents out around their house doing odd jobs.

Now with the six children born prior to this one, a person could only guess that the money was tight and food was somewhat scarce. Because this most important event happened on November 25, 1944, there wasn't any money for a Thanksgiving turkey. I weighed twelve pounds at birth and was jokingly referred to as a twelve-pound Thanksgiving turkey. This is one of the stories I have always heard from my elders. It has stayed with me even today.

Being born the seventh child and weighing twelve pounds, which had to cause my mom a lot of pain and grief, has to mean something of importance. As the story goes, I became a chubby little boy and somehow became very adored as a baby by the older women in the labor camp. It seemed that they wanted to hold me constantly. But, when I was around eighteen months old, I've been told, my mom and dad packed up all their belongings, including us seven kids, and headed west once again.

I am not sure if the vegetable season came to an end or if my dad just got restless for a cooler promised land. The small tent-trailer that the parents had when leaving the dust bowl of Oklahoma years earlier was now really crowded. I'm also not sure what type of navigation the parents used to guide them during these early years, but somehow, we stopped in a small California town in Tulare County called Terra Bella.

This town then was essentially a farm labor town with a grocery store, a soda fountain, a variety store, a single doctor, an elementary school, a citrus packing shed, and about four churches. In this town, life was going to be great (for me). My mom and dad were both working, and I had five older sisters and one older brother to take care of me and be at my baby-beckoning call. What a life I was going to have in this town.

My sisters cared for my needs the best way they could. About January 1947, my mom got sick as I recall. It may have been the old flu symptoms again, somewhat like before. When my parents returned from getting treatment and medication, I knew nothing of what was wrong with her. My family made me wait for nine long months to see what the doctor had told my mom and dad

It was October 1948 when the eighth stork landed on our doorstep with a little brother for me to play with. When I asked the stork, he said he was still tired after delivering the other seven kids. My mom suggested the name Wayne. So the name suggested stuck, and number eight became Wayne. Later, I realized that my mom and dad went to a town about twenty miles north of Terra Bella called Porterville and asked the tired stork to stop by our house with his special delivery package. With this special "D," there were eight kids now, and we were getting more crowded in the small two-bedroom house in which all ten, including my mom and dad lived. It seemed that the family was large enough.

As mentioned above, my dad and a few neighbors built this two-bedroom brick house. As I recall, it had a kitchen and a living room. The plumbing for the house was way back in the corner of the half-acre lot. I assume that the family stayed in a tent while the construction was going on. I am not sure where we all slept except for my mom and dad. They had their own bedroom. I had to sleep with my older brother on the added-on back porch. He was six years older than me. I don't think I had to sleep with "special D," however.

On the other half acre, there were summer fruit trees: one peach, one apricot, one apple, and one plum. There was a nectarine tree and even a small vine near the back fence that had grapes on it every August. Each of the fruits had a very sweet taste when it was ripe. I can't recall having to pick up any rotten or spoiled ones. After settling, my dad worked with a man who lived just down the street and on the corner from our brick house. The Browning family became the first family that my parents met and became friends with after moving to California. This family friendship lasted up to the time of death of all members to date.

While living in the brick house I began eating dirt, whether brown, blackened with oil, or red in color. Not sure if it was tasty, but I seem to enjoy it. I am not sure why I did this. It wasn't because of the lack of food. We did have plenty.

Like a lot of kids with nothing much to do, one day I threw dirt clods (chunks of dirt similar to a snowballs) at the three or four cars that passed our house. The first couple of drivers either didn't see me throw the dirt clod or knew there would be no damage, so they continued on with their journey.

I wasn't so lucky when the last car came by. I carefully aimed a projectile (which would break into thousands of very small dust like pieces when it collided with the asphalt). As the car got directly even with me, I let go of this weapon and watched as it exploded and the dirt pieces went in all directions. Some went under the car, and some went behind the car. What a good throw; seeing the dirt spread out all over gave me a thrill of success. Until the car came to a stop and backed up. I remember thinking, *"Why is that car stopping? I didn't get it dirty."*

Just as I was finishing my thought, a Goliath-sized man came walking around the rear of the car and came toward me with a mean, stern look. He said something, but I didn't hear what he was saying because my nerves and fright were yelling at me so loud that it was hard to hear anything. I think he said, "Why are you throwing dirt at my car?" and something about how I better stop. I apologized and assured him that I would not do it again.

As he got back into his car and drove away, I heard a small clicking sound. Looking down, I noticed my knees were slapping each other. Being frightened, I was glad that he was gone. Needless to say, the last clod had been thrown.

Across the dirt and grassy field behind our small house was a small Pentecostal church that we began attending on a very regular basis. Because I was too young and probably involved in my own world, I can recall only two things about our attendance.

The first thing I remember is the booster band, which was made up of the children of the folks who attended services there. After Sunday school classes, we would be called to the stage in front of the building and in front of everyone. We would be seated, although I am not sure if the seating was assigned or what. The band began harmonizing at the direction of the pastor. Each one of us had a Bible verse that we said each Sunday. One girl had the verse "Jesus wept," and my verse was "God is love." As the rotation of group continued, the verses were spoken. Each child was nervous as he or she be recited the verse. When the band was finished performing, as a reward for our job well done, each band member got to choose a gift from a woven basket. The gifts were a selection of balloons, small penny candies, or a paper toy. I always looked for a dime or quarter at the bottom of the basket—no luck.

The second thing that I remember about this small church was that my family, excluding my dad, attended together. The older sisters, Virginia, Colleen, and Lois, would sing together once or twice a month in a group and perform a special song of their choosing. I remember they each wore a blouse and skirt to match. On a few occasions, the oldest of the eight kids, Betty June, would help deliver the special song, and she also played her tambourine as they sang. I don't remember what songs they sang, but I do remember seeing them in front of everyone on this stage the singing their hearts out and sounding like nightingales.

After the service every Sunday, we would walk back across the field, being careful not to snag our clothes on the weeds and grass. Back at our brick house, one fine and sunny day when

I was about five years old, I was in the front yard playing. To my surprise, I saw a small Shetland horse coming down our street with his owner. I really like horses, as most kids do at my age. The owner talked to my mom for a few minutes. The next thing I knew I had a cowboy hat on my head and a red scarf tied around my neck, and I was ready to ride. The older fellow set me on the horse and told me his name was Sparky. That name didn't fit him at all. This pony was either too old or too tired or didn't want to have anybody sitting on top of his back. I thought I was about two stories high sitting on Sparky. I was so high that I had to hold on to the small saddle horn so I wouldn't fall off. Shortly after putting on my cowboy hat and scarf and getting in the saddle, I was ready.

I was ready for the ride that I'd always wanted. Sparky's friend pulled out a black box and set it on a three-legged stick. My mom told me to sit still. It was then that I knew I would not be riding anywhere. This older guy was going to take a picture or two of me as if I was riding like a cowboy.

It is sure not what I expected. If I wouldn't have been so scared, I would have gently kicked Sparky in the sides and rode off into the sunset. The pictures turned out good, and somehow I still have one of me being a cowboy hanging on the wall.

No one in my family was aware of my affair with the housewife across the street that I had. My sister Carol was friends with her daughter, Barbara. I was probably four or five years old when the affair began. It started one day when the newspaper was delivered to her front yard. With nothing much to do in the neighborhood, I went across the street, picked up her paper so that it wouldn't get wet from the damp grass, and went to the back door and knocked. This was the first time that I had ever done anything like this. My heart was throbbing and about to pop out when Mrs. Cassman came to answer the door.

I handed her the dry paper and told her that I didn't want it to get wet. She then asked me to come in, and she set me down on a stool in the kitchen area. Then it happened. She asked me, "Would you like a cookie?" I said please, and we talk for a short time while I ate and savored the treat. It sure tasted better than the dirty dirt. What four- or five-year-old wouldn't enjoy a delicious cookie? That's how the affair began. Every day I would wait for the newspaper to arrive on the lawn. I would deliver it to the back door and enjoy a cookie.

On the southeast corner, just south of our brick house, lived a childhood friend. Randy had a sister who was blind. Linda seemed to always know when I would enter their house to do whatever we were going to do. She had a remarkable ability to know who was visiting. So one day I had just enough courage to ask her how she knew it was me each time. I was so shocked and left almost speechless when she told me that she recognized my voice. At the age I was, I had never known a person who was blind or had any other type of disability. Not being aware of this, I was pleasantly surprised.

About four or five houses east of Linda's, a small brick house sat back off the road in the middle of the property lot. In this house lived one of the sweetest older ladies who always had a fresh fruit pie cooked or a delicious cake sitting on the table just waiting for friends to sit down and enjoy the delicious flavor. This older lady was my dad's only sister, Ann. Boy, I sure did enjoy going over to her house. It always smelled delicious as the aroma of something being cooked drifted throughout the rooms, grabbed hold of you as you entered, wrapped its inviting aroma around you, and led you to a chair where an empty plate sat waiting for you on the table.

My aunt also had an old-fashioned water pump in the backyard. It seemed to sit there just waiting for some thirsty person to come by for a small amount of water and prime it, and it would give you gallons as needed of very cold, fresh water. The water was pumped into a pale or bucket and carried into the house for all to enjoy and be refreshed. She had a metal cup that had a long handle about twelve inches long to dip out a cup of clear freshness for all. Now thinking back over the years, knowing that my aunt showered her love and affection for everyone through her cooking and baking, I don't recall her ever hugging me or telling me that she loved me. I always knew she did because of the small things she did.

About three or four houses to the east and on the other side of the street lived a lady whom I didn't know much about but later found out that she was my dad's aunt. I mentioned Great-Aunt Minnie here because she lived close and I didn't get to know her very well. Her branch of the family tree had some interesting branches and events and people that I'll write about later in chapters to come.

Continuing eastward down the street you could find the Bishop family on the north side of the street. On the south side, closer to the railroad tracks, was the Poplin family. Also next to the railroad tracks was a large orange citrus packing shed that employed the majority of the residents of the town. I believe my mom and sisters worked there seasonally.

On the corner of the street that ran parallel to the railroad tracks was the town square where a person could find the soda fountain, the variety store, a grocery store, and a few other stores. I cannot recall what types they were, and neither can my elders. Don't blink as we continue through the streets, however.

On the right side near the city square was Dr. Johnson's office, where everyone in town went to have their illnesses taking care of. The post office was next to Dr. Johnson's office.

A person could get medical treatment and mail a letter or pick up mail with one stop.

A few grade school friends, including Dickie Dickerson, lived in the apartment building close to the post office. Just before you went down the little hill, on the right and on the corner, stood (and probably still stands) an Episcopal church.

The most exciting venue of this area in Terra Bella was next to the Episcopal church—the elementary school. I have every fond memories of the small school and the three years I attended. First day in 1949, when I was almost ready for high school at age five, my mom helped to introduce me to a whole new world of life. It was a world full of strangers, things to do (which looked very inviting), and rows of metal legs with white-looking smooth wood tops. I wasn't sure if I wanted or was ready for a new world with all these weird things and the flat wood tops.

As I recall, the first day was occupied with the adults getting to know our names and putting each of the other munchkins in a flattop (much like my older brothers' hairstyles). The adults didn't seem to care if we knew the munchkin in front or behind us. About the second day, one at a time, each munchkin had to stand in front of the others and tell everyone his or her name, what the dad did for work, and a little about him- or herself. Telling my name and something about myself came somewhat easier than telling that my parents were farm laborers. Little did I know at the time that the majority of the parents were working on a farm or a ranch. So as most munchies will do, the truth about the work my parents did became as a rubber band (i.e., it stretched out the facts some and will return to the truth or true size). None of the other munchies knew that the rubber band theory had been used, but probably did realize the truth later.

As I made a few friends, each day seemed to be more fun. I did have a fun-filled time at school. So much find that I can't remember if I learned anything except when it was time for recess and lunch. I had those times engraved in my mind so deep. When the following school year began to approach, the teachers notified my parents (who lacked school learning) that a conference of sort was needed to discuss my progress, or lack thereof, in the first grade. The teacher must have told my mom, because my dad rarely went to anything relating to education. She noted how I had excelled in what I was good at, which was recess and lunchtime. She recommended that because I did not attend kindergarten, I should not be passed into the second grade but remain in the first grade to learn what had been taught. I was on the honor roll for recess and lunch. So when the news spread and the second graders would ask, I would again use the rubber band theory and tell them that the teacher needed a knowledgeable assistant to help her out. They sure were gullible.

Chapter 3

The summer of 1949 occurred after the first grade. Also during that hot summer, one of the many disasters in my life happened. It seemed to sneak up on me. Without warning or preparation, my mom and dad packed everything in our house, which wasn't much in today's standards, and we moved north about twenty miles to another town also in Tulare County called Porterville.

The reason this surprise move was so disastrous for me was I had to start all over again. My teacher in Terra Bella already knew that I liked recess and lunch better, that I did not like to work too hard, and that I didn't know how to study or do homework. This new teacher, who had been teaching for about sixty years, would not know anything about me. I didn't even know when recess time was at this new school. I knew lunchtime was always about the same time every day. What was I going to do? How was I going to deal with this disaster?

Well, about once or twice a week, the class would participate in show-and-tell. I would never have anything to show anyone, and I didn't have anything to tell (unless it was recess or lunchtime). One day I recalled the rubber band theory and how it seemed to work before the great disaster occurred to me. I couldn't be the only kid in class who had nothing to show or tell about. So the next time we had a show-and-tell I had to have a story. I just couldn't be left out.

Because my four older sisters were married, that meant that I had four brothers-in-law who either had been in or were still in the military. In the military, they wore a uniform I was very impressed with even as a six-year-old munchkin, so my show-and-tell story was that my dad was going to buy me a uniform. Each week the uniform was from a different branch of the military. I was only familiar with two or three branches at that time. The show part of my show-and-tell never came to be. I was afraid that rubber band theory would stretch too far and break.

However, one week, show-and-tell was the uniform, and for the following weeks, my dad bought the military cap, medals, etc. The stories made the air so thick I could hardly walk back to my desk. The thickness of the air was like the Chicago air in the hot summertime with its heavy humidity.

Even though Mrs. Corzine probably didn't believe my military stories at show-and-tell time, I'm sure she was very glad to sign the slip that had the words *second grade* on it. She knew how my parents were struggling with all eight of us at home before the older sisters began to marry and start their own lives.

The rubber band theory must have been destroyed and the rubber band broken when I entered the second grade. The second grade was uneventful, as I recall, until later in the year when I met the twins.

Eddie and Teddy were the brothers of one of my oldest brother's best friends. As it happened, the twins and I became friends and sort of hung out together when at school. The twins and I moved on to the third grade together. The second-grade teacher was probably glad to see us move on up.

Sometime during the third grade year (about 1952), the three of us came to be known as the three musketeers. We discovered an interest that we had, which continued on through to the fourth grade. This mutual interest was running. We became an early Forrest Gump. Although all three of us ran, we became competitive, even with each other. We would not run the streets but in grass and fields at Burton Elementary School every moment we could get. I am not sure of the education I received. There had to be some there, because after the long summer after the third grade, the musketeers would all be found sitting near each other in the fourth grade.

Now, the fourth grade was a very different approach to education for me. Things were getting more serious and harder and resulting in schoolwork that we had to complete and return the next day. During this fourth grade year, I'm not sure why, but I became interested in attempting to develop any skills I might have in music. So I took a violin off the shelf and started playing. In high school, I later found that any musical talent in me that might have had a glimmer of a chance was vocal.

I guess that interest of the three musketeers was somewhat stronger. Eddie, Teddy, and I kept on running during the fourth grade. Each time we competed against each other, Eddie was just a little faster. While I was almost touching Eddie's heels, Teddy was almost touching mine.

The musketeers became such good friends that they would invite me over to spend the night, usually on a Friday or Saturday. To their surprise, I went home with them one weekday after school. After some playing outside, we went inside for a delicious dinner. I am not sure exactly what was on the menu that night, but I do recall their mom was a really good cook. After dinner, we sat down to relax and watch *The*

Mickey Mouse Club on TV. Just before dark, there was a knock on their front door.

A salesperson seemed to always be coming around to sell his wares and goods during this time in the evening when everyone was home, just as they do today. The twins' dad opened the door to see what was being offered for sale. There was a person standing in the evening light, which made it difficult to see the person's face. When I did see, I was hoping it was my mom's twin. Really fast, my pea-sized memory recalled that my mom had many sisters but no twins.

Oh no! I remember thinking. *I forgot. I forgot to ask or let my mom know about my musketeer adventure at the twins' house after school.*

However, after she rescued her brave one from his misadventure, she continued to let me know she was worried during the mile or so that we had to walk home. She had to look everyplace; she asked a lot of people who might know her musketeer and tried to find out where the twins lived. I don't think she even attempted to listen to any of my excuses. Besides, with the belt that she had in her hand and just knowing that I would be feeling it shortly, I must have come up with a lot of excuses.

Still being a little sore the next day, I knew that I would never forget to tell my mom with the black two-and-a-half-inch belt where I was going or where I would be in the future. I did learn a valuable lesson that day. The union of the musketeer's— one for all and all for one—came to pass with the school ending that school year.

One day my mom had a conference with Mrs. Ellis, my fourth-grade teacher, just before the school year ended. It seems that Mrs. Ellis must have needed a trusty assistant to help her during the next school year. She chose me. As the twins and others asked why I wasn't in their classroom, I told them of my new assistant job. At the time, I was too ashamed to let them know that I was being kept back. I would not be able to run with them in the fifth grade.

While living in the all-American city of Porterville during my first-grade year through about the fifth grade, we attended a small church on the corner of E Street and Orange Avenue. As a youngster, attending a Saturday night service at church caused the day to become very long. So what does a child of young years do when his bedtime arrives even at church on a Saturday night? The child will find a bed, or a lap, to take a nap on.

This was the case on many occasions for me. One of these bedtime events came about while I was napping on the front pew during the pastor's sermon. He must have been delivering a message on not paying attention or falling asleep. During his preaching, he woke me up when he took my arm and stood me up in front of the entire congregation and continued talking. Because I could not wake up, I had no idea what his message was about or why he woke me up like that.

Another event that gave me a shock was when my younger brother wanted to go to the nearby rails and climb on the railcars after Sunday school. The three railcars were close because of the packing sheds that were nearby. We had played on the railroad cars before and got into trouble when we returned after church service with dirty clothes. On this particular Sunday, we were going to be smart when playing on the railcars and not get our clothes dirty. We carefully climbed on the top of the cars, looked around from our elevated position to see what things looked like from these cars, and then ran over to the second car. On this particular day, there was a third car. As we jumped to the third one, we heard a voice calling. Because the railcars are much wider then we were tall, we had to walk over to the edge to see who was calling.

Thinking it was our dad returning from visiting cousins to pick us up after church service, we were really surprised when we saw a city policeman staring up at us. Our legs seemed to be a little weak as we climbed down the ladder that was attached to the side of the railcar. As our feet touched the ground, the officer lined us up and questioned us about what we were doing. My little brother told him we were playing. The officer's second question was something like, "Where do you belong?"

When we told him the church, he said, "Get back over there. There is no playing on these railcars."

Strangely, that was the last time we did that.

Chapter 4

A second disaster occurred to me after completing the fourth grade at Burton Elementary School. I knew nothing about it until after it happened. When I did finally find out, I was both glad and yet unhappy.

The second disaster was that my parents sold the house in Porterville, which had a radio and TV repair shop, and moved back to Terra Bella. In some respects, the move returning to friends in the quaint small town of Terra Bella was exciting. However, I knew I would not only miss my friends, but I would miss working with my dad in the repair shop. After all, I had been for four long years. But the downfall of this return was that we moved into an olive orchard that was about two or three miles west of town.

The year was about 1955, and I was a kid of about eleven years old. How was I going to go into town to visit the friends whom we'd left a few years before? One day, as a beam of light entered into my brain, I had this idea that I would walk or ride my first bike, which I'd bought from Roger, our neighbor in Porterville. That's exactly what I did a few times.

The reason my parents moved the family back to the Terra Bella area was that my dad had accepted a managerial position for the olive company that he was working for. I stayed with my third sister and her family for about a month during the move back. My family lived in the middle of this olive orchard for about a year. During this exciting, single year, my dad taught me to drive two different kinds of tractors. One was a crawler type with tracks (like a military tank). The second tractor had four wheels. Boy, they were fun!!

I learned some about olive tree ranching and the care it takes to keep trees producing fruit each year. I also had a lot of fun playing and pretending among the trees and in the fields. During the fall harvest, I was able to practice what I had learned about the tractors. As I turned a corner to continue picking up the boxes of picked olives, the front of the wheel tractor struck a stack of full boxes and caused a spill. Needless to say, I had to clean up the spill. My uncle came by to see what was going on. Jokingly, he told me that the olives were placed in a can after being picked and cleaned. I love olives and could not resist tasting a fresh one. The joke was on me. Olives just picked off the tree are very bitter. They have to go through the brimming process in order to be tasty and packed in a can or jar for the market.

One day after harvest, I was going to ride my twenty-four-inch bike the couple of miles to visit some cousins who lived near town. To my dismay, my younger sibling had used my bike and seemed to find a patch of goat heads or stickers, and you can guess what had happened. The tires—both of them—were flat. Still feeling the need to go, I walk the distance to town.

Of course, I had to stop at the corner fountain. Because I did not have any money and it was hot, I had to ask for a cool class of water. On one of my walks to town, I stopped to visit Dick, my friend who had just broken his arm the week before. The arm had a slight bend to it that prevented him from completely straightening his arm. I can't remember exactly what we did other than just hang out.

Another time I went to town using my shoes as transportation to visit Marcello and Blanca, who were also elementary school friends. The few times I visited my cousins, the Poplins, we had to investigate the goings on at the orange-packing shed when it was closed for the day.

The small farming town of Terra Bella had the best elementary school. I started the fifth grade when we moved back. Living in this county did create a few difficulties for me, however. The first was that I would have to get up and out of bed a little earlier to wait for the school bus. The second was that I had to, most importantly, get back on the same school bus after school to go for a long ride home. The third was that I couldn't hang out with any friends after school unless I wanted to walk home.

I do remember what happened when I went home with Eddie and Teddy after school. So I chose not to visit any friends after school unless I asked my parents first. The teacher at Terra Bella Elementary for the fifth grade was a male teacher named E. R. Armstrong. Mr. Armstrong almost always made learning a lot of fun. He used contests, spelling bees, and map games to aid him in teaching and help the students with learning. I seemed to be good with map geography and spelling. I was the first to get to the front of the room when geography or spelling subjects time came up.

On a few occasions, David Brown's mom would make a surprise visit to the classroom. The surprise was always for the students and seemed to be on a day of a spelling bee or map geography. On those days, the class was usually in an active mode, which would allow Mrs. Brown and Mr. Armstrong a little time to talk. We had extra time to enjoy the pan full of chocolate brownies that she surprised us with. I bet we made a mess of the classroom.

One week Mr. Armstrong must have been sick. The class had to struggle with a substitute teacher who sure wasn't as much fun as Mr. Armstrong. One of the days when she was putting all of us through the education paces, Ronnie Browning, a neighborhood friend, and I began putting our right index fingers on the inside of our left jaw would wrap that in tip of the finger along the inside of the jaw. As the finger would slip out past the lips and with a little pressure applied to the finger, a popping sound would break the silence in the classroom. By the time the substitute teacher would look up or turn around to investigate the cause of this loud pop noise, she would find both Ronnie and I very busy working on whatever project or lesson we were supposed to be doing. Many of the students continually laughed, which had to irritate the teacher.

The second or third day she began to zero in on this horrible sound and found us with sore jaws and talking sort of funny. What could she do? Because Ronnie knew the way to the school office, I let him lead the way down a very long cement walkway, which seemed to lead directly to a large brown door with a sign that said "School Office.'" After slithering through the brown door, we had to sit into chairs.

I guess it was not to wait for the next game to play but to see some person of importance. When that man finally came out, I wasn't sure if I really wanted to meet or talk to him. I found out from Ronnie that this man was the principal of the school. The room where we waited for him looked like any other room with a couple of tables and some books on shelves. I realized a lot later the wait was to let us sweat some and worry a lot about what we were in the office for. Because we both had to wait and Ronnie knew what was going to happen, that knowledge amplified everything. (As a side note, in the nineteen fifties and with the approval of parents, a principal had permission to swat children a couple of times.) In our case, our parents knew the principal quite well. Because Ronnie had been down this path before and had knowledge of this process, he began putting thin hardback books inside his pants and under his shirt, which were held in place by his belt. Suddenly, the door to our room opened, and the feared principal approached us.

With his evil look, he asked, "Who wants to be first?"

I am so glad that Ronnie volunteered to be first to suffer the pain-wrenching swats that were about to be inflicted on us. As Ronnie entered the separate room and the door slammed closed behind him, I began to listen very intensely. I finally put my ear against the door to magnify any sound that I anticipated. It's funny—I did not hear any sound, so I really began to wonder what was going happening on the other side of the door. It seemed like an hour later when the door opened again, and I was directed to enter the other room. *Oh man!* I thought. *I was so busy listening that I forgot to place any books or other protection in my pants.*

What was going to happen? To my dismay and relief, this once-scary principal must have had a change of heart for us. After he spoke to us in a firm tone and we agreed to discontinue the annoying popping sounds, he allowed us to return to the classroom and humbly apologize to the substitute teacher for disturbing the class. We were so happy and our bottoms felt better about the swats that were never to be.

One of the things that I appreciated about moving back to the small farming town was that we finally had indoor plumbing at the olive ranch house. The house was provided by the Pacific Olive Company for the manager and his family while working for them.

While living in Porterville as mentioned earlier, we had an old, smelly outhouse. We lived there for four years; it had to be moved once that I recall. I can't remember who dug the hole, which was probably about five-foot square and seven feet deep. After the hole was dug, the wooden structure was set over it. Not sure who did all this, but it happened. This outhouse was set out almost in the middle of our three-quarter of an acre of land. To keep this house company, we also had a calf to keep the grass mowed down.

The indoor plumbing in the ranch house was a welcomed change. The aroma in the house and the convenience was a great improvement. Another small thing that was good about the ranch was that we were able to have chickens, which resulted in fresh eggs and fresh chicken for the table at mealtime. We also had a large garden that produced as much of every kind of vegetables that we could take care of. What a great treat to go out and get a fresh veggie that you helped to grow. After the fifth grade year at this small and inspiring town, another devastating occurrence happened that actually changed my life.

BEFORE I TELL you about this next devastating event, I must tell you about a visit out on the ranch. As I recall, I started the fifth grade at Terra Bella Elementary. One Saturday, a longtime friend of my dad's, Art and his wife, Duchess, stopped by to visit. Wayne and I continue playing and chasing the animals outside. They stayed for about an hour. I am sure my parents had a conversation afterward. I believe the visit from the longtime friends was about the amount of hard work and responsibility that dad had and led to the decision that was made, which change my life.

Chapter 5

It was approximately February or March 1956 when we, once again, moved. This move was about three and a half hours north to a quaint little town in Stanislaus County. My dad had purchased a thirty-eight-foot trailer house, which would be our fall and winter home. He found a farm labor camp in Empire that had some space available. That is where the trailer was parked.

This labor camp had both mobile trailers and long rows of apartments that people rented. My dad's brother Sam and his wife lived in one of the apartments. After a few months, my aunt Ann moved into one also. Aunt Ann had an aroma of something delicious that drifted throughout the house, wrapped around you, and almost sent you to a chair at the table. So guess where I hung out a lot.

There are a lot of memories that came out of the labor camp during the ten or eleven years we lived there during the fall and winter months. One of the memories that pops into my pea brain is that as a preteen and teenager the boys and I thought we were the coolest. We walked around with our hair greased down and the sleeves of our white T-shirts rolled up. The rolls were too tight to put a pack of cigarettes in, however. When we were not being so cool, about six of us would each roll an old, worn-out car tire down the half-dirt, half-asphalt-with-chuck-holes road to have something to do for entertainment.

Someone probably complained or said something to Roy, the labor camp manager. One day as we rolled our tires around the holes in the road, guess who we saw coming. Roy made us put our game tires in a storage room adjacent to the laundry room located almost in the middle of the camp. Of course, the boys didn't want our tires to be lonely in this cold, dark room. What else could we do?

One of the guys went through the small screen that was over the side window and opened the door that Roy had used so we could rescue our game tires. Strangely enough, we were not bothered again. He never did ask us about the escape of the tires.

The second facility was near one of the front entrances to the camp. These communal facilities were used every day after working at the job or in the fields by the person who lived there. On the north end of each building was a laundry room with three or four washers and dryers.

Also near the center building was a picnic-type table and bench. When there was no rain and daily work was finished, the senior man of this camp would gather and play game after game after game of dominoes and occasionally cards.

One of the things I recall about this labor camp from earlier years was that while we actually lived in Porterville and Terra Bella during the winters, we would travel north to various areas to help harvest crops during the summers. We traveled those earlier years with a small two-wheel trailer and carried supplies as in the very early years before I was born when my parents left Oklahoma searching for a promised land.

When we arrived at this labor camp, the older siblings unloaded the tent and set it up. Some years we would have access to a wooden frame to attach the cloth tent to. This wooden skeletal structure also had a wooden floor. Some years the tent was set up on the ground. One year we were fortunate enough to be able to stretch our tent on to one of the four wooden structures. Somehow, one year my arm became infected and inflamed. It was painful and pus filled and swollen. This is mostly commonly known as a boil. Dr. Dad and Dr. Mom, of course, using old home remedies, purchased a large bag of raisins and had me eat them until I could not eat anymore. I recall eating and eating. I thought I was becoming a raisin the night of the eating marathon. My doctors' theory was that the raisins would purify the blood, and the condition would heal itself. I am not sure if the raisins helped any, but after a week or so, my arm became pain free and the swelling was gone. Before the cure, one morning I as woke up, I noticed that there were black creepy crawlers in the bag of raisins. The ants had taken over. I knew that the raisin-eating time was over.

A permanent move to Empire meant I had to make new friends and start another school, which really scared me. Finding my way around, although I had done it before, was going to be a big challenge for me because my older sisters had the responsibility of caring for the younger siblings. They gave me the responsibility of playing with and overseeing the safety of my younger brother when they did the household chores.

The first day at this new school my parents went off to work early. Those who worked on a farm or labored in the fields always went to work at a very early hour each morning before the heat of the day.

On this first day of school, not knowing where my sister was, I knew I had to get our younger brother out of bed, make up the bunks beds, help him with putting his clothes on, and fix our breakfast. Afterward, I washed our dishes, along with the ones my parents left in the sink. The linoleum floors had to be swept also. My mom would be too tired after working all day.

After walking a mile or so to school, I had to register both of us into school. Wayne was in the second grade, and I was in the sixth. This process was performed each school morning. My older sisters had always done what they could to help the family in the past, and I was no different. The same blood runs deep.

This move to this new life must have been made during the early spring, after Art and his wife visited my parents at the olive ranch. The first school year at Empire Union Elementary ended in the middle of June that next year. Every summer until I was a junior in high school, my dad would hook up the smaller pull trailer that we had and travel to the northern states to harvest the prized fruit of the area where we would stop.

The first partial year at Empire Union wasn't any different. Upon arriving in The Dalles, Oregon, this particular year, I had to write Empire Union Elementary School to request my report card in case I had to start a different school. The report card was sent to me in The Dalles with a note that said something like, "Since you were not at Empire union long enough to be graded on subjects, we are sending your report card from the last school you attended." The continual moving around, leaving friends, and starting different schools did affect my life in a negative way. However, I learned and became stronger from the experiences.

We worked picking Bing cherries in Oregon. The job at this location lasted three or four weeks. Just before we were finished with cleaning these trees of the dark-red, delicious fruit of this first year, I was in the top of this giant tree. Something very weird began.

The birds stopped chirping and singing as a dark shadow

began to appear very slowly. It seemed to be covering everything in its path. I wondered what in the world was going on. Because I was in the very top of the tree, I wanted to get a bird's-eye view what was happening. I knew it was unusual and not natural for it to be so dark in the middle of the day. When I looked up from the very top of this huge tree, I saw what appeared to be something trying to either turn the sunlight off or something covering the sun like a blanket. As this blanket slowly moved over the sun, the light came on in this pea brain of mine and I realized that the moon was passing between the sun and the earth. The light of the sun was turned off for a moment, and as the moon blanket was slowly removed, the light of day returned. The birds sang a different song, and I returned to work.

The second school year at Empire Union when I was in the seventh grade was uneventful. It was the same old boring stuff to a fourteen-year-old. Once again, when school was out for the summer, it was the same performance. My dad had the small trailer hooked and wired up and ready to return to our summer travels. Again we traveled to The Dalles, Oregon, to do the same thing as we had done the previous year. That year we didn't have the total eclipse, but there was some kid excitement waiting for me. If I recall correctly, we completed the harvest, got paid, and a few days before we had to leave for our next destination to the big sky State of Montana, we all went fishing.

It seems that there is a very large river similar to the mighty Mississippi River that softly flows between the states of Oregon and Washington. The Columbia River has two or three dams on it, and one of these dams is in The Dallas, Oregon. This dam is very large and entertains the salmon as they fight to go upstream (which makes no sense to me) to spawn and lay their eggs for a beginning of a new generation.

Living and playing in this large river is the sturgeon. This fish is also a food fish and a valuable source of caviar. At my age, I had no idea about this and probably would not have cared about caviar. I was more interested in catching a fish. So we went fishing in the great Columbia River. After teaching my worm to swim gracefully, he went for the swim of his life.

It seemed that twelve hours passed by, but it was actually about thirty minutes. The war on the end of my line let me know that his worm dance enticed a fish to take a bite of him. As this fish took his first bite, I reeled him to the river bank. He seemed to be willing, because he didn't put up a fight. He just floated in; for me, getting him out of the water was a trick. Before placing my prize—the largest fish I ever caught—into a water container to hold him, the fish had to be measured.

There was a law that a sturgeon fish had to be between thirty-six and seventy-two inches in order to keep it. Otherwise, he would be able to rejoin the branch on his family tree. To me, this fish was mine. He had to be at least forty or fifty inches. He was the biggest one that I had ever caught.

My dad and another man came over to where I was. The two helped measure this beast. He looked like a baby whale he was so big. As the measuring tape rolled out of its casing, it stopped at thirty-five and half inches. I had my dad re-measure to make sure the other man was measuring right. He had probably never used a measuring tape. The second measurement came out and extended to another thirty-five and half inches. *You've got to be kidding!* I thought.

I asked Dad if, since we were from another state, the half inch could be overlooked At least I tried. Reluctantly, I sent the thirty-five and half-inch fish back to his family to grow until I returned the following year.

The next school year would be my last at Empire Union. It was a good school, but I guess all the staff was tired of trying to teach the unteachable. So after this last year, they gave me a ceremony (along with the entire eighth grade class) on a Wednesday evening. I guess they were also tired of all the eighth-grade class. We all received a ceremony before we had to leave.

A couple of days after the graduation, we again left to go north. That year, when the Oregon work was done, my dad hooked the small trailer again, and we headed for the big sky state of Montana. I always enjoyed the trips, the scenery, and the chance to meet other people. When we arrived in Montana, we stopped at the south shore of beautiful Flat Head Lake in the western region of the huge state. What I really remember about the city of Polson was the twenty-five-cent movie theater and the ice cream stand on the corner near where we were parked with our trailer. We stopped at the same place for the three years that we traveled to Montana. I will always remember the town of Polson. It was there that I received my first kiss. I was sixteen. Denise was a surprise to me. She did teach me the art well.

On one of the trips, my younger brother Wayne and I went to the twenty-five-cent movie and watched the Glenn Miller story—what a great story. The family also went to the North Shore of Flat Head Lake to the town of Kalispell and stopped at the Thompson Lakes for a few days. While fishing one day, a total stranger drove up to the dock and asked if anyone wanted to go for a ride. The stranger seemed to be nice, so a few of the younger set got in the boat for a ride. This stranger instructed me on the safety of driving a boat. The owner instructed me on the proper operation of the boat and let me drive for a while. I was nervous. This was my first time to be in a boat, and I had the responsibility of the passengers

A day or two later, we loaded up and drove westward through the town of Libby and on into Idaho. I recall beginning the eighth grade in Fruitland Elementary School in Idaho. The fruit harvest was late, and my parents wanted to finish the job before we went back to California. After arriving at Gay Way Junction across the Snake River from Ontario, Oregon, Dad decided we should make a trip to South Dakota to visit my third sister Colleen and her family.

I was fifteen, and I guess my dad wanted to test my skills at controlling a vehicle. Of course, I had driver's permit, so he let me drive across Idaho going through Twin Falls and Idaho Falls on Freeway 84 and across Wyoming and on into Hot Springs, South Dakota. While enjoying the cool summer weather of that area, we were treated to a visit to Mount Rushmore and a dinosaur museum on top in a small mountain that overlooked Rapid City.

After our visit, I guess we returned to Gay Way Junction. I don't remember the return trip at all because I didn't get to drive. When it was time to for school to start, my younger brother and I began school in Fruitland. Fruitland, as I recall, was a small farm labor town. I felt that I would not do well in school there, probably because of my insecurity. Everything seemed to be too different from what I was used to. The calming that I had during the short time we were there was I met Bonnie. Bonnie was a cute, black-haired girl who caught my eye. She worked in the cafeteria each day. That is when I was able to see her and get a smile. Because we were both bashful and shy, we didn't say much to each other. She as the one whom I missed when we moved back to California.

Back in California, we would get settled in to our routine. Attend school during the week, work on Saturdays helping my dad with the job he had going on that week, get paid, and move on to the next job. During the summer of 1962, I worked hard and somehow saved almost all the money I made all summer long.

When we returned to our home base of Modesto at the end of the summer that year, my dad and uncle took me to Oakland to find my very first car. After arriving in Oakland, we drove and looked and then drove and looked some more. Finally, I saw a 1950, two-door hardtop Chevy that I had to have. With the dark mint-green body and black top, nobody in the big Valley would have one like mine. We bought it, and even though I had a driver's license, I lacked the experience, so my uncle drove the car home. I rode shotgun. What a surreal moment, knowing this car was mine and I'd paid cash for it.

At school, with my 1950 Chevy, I became very popular. Everyone wanted to be my friend. It didn't take too long for me to learn to things. First, these guys weren't my friends, and second, although I didn't want to accept it, my new car would not run without fuel in the tank. This last realization meant responsibility came, and the decision had to be made between toys and a car.

My dad introduced me to work that wasn't in the summertime. Walt Henley, a local peach rancher, was having my dad do some work for his elderly mom about three days a week. My parents also purchased slightly cracked eggs at a nearby chicken ranch in order to save some money. My dad told me about the yard work, and my mom referred me to the chicken ranch.

One day my mom mentioned something to the chicken rancher about her sixteen-year-old son having just bought a car. I guess she just might have used the rubber band theory. A week later he gave me a job working on alternating days. I learned to feed all the chickens and gather eggs while on an electric-powered gathering machine. The manager Don even gave me the most honored job on the ranch. Little did I know that even with chickens, when food goes in, poop is the result.

One of my jobs was shoveling the perfume-ridden mess. Using a wheelbarrow, I had to wheel it out to the peach field next to the ranch and dump it. The most fun came every winter when the weather was cold and wet. My job process became liquefied and lots of fun to move. After a couple of seasons on the ranch, I was able to talk to a close friend's dad. He was a deacon at the church I attended, and he was also the owner of a Flying A full-service station.

The sad part of finding a new job was telling the boss that I was leaving. Another part was telling my aging dad that I couldn't travel north anymore to help work in the harvest. He understood that my help would not be forever. Though he was disappointed, I think he accepted the fact that I was accepting of my responsibilities and was easing into manhood. He was sixty years old at the time and chose to retire. He knew that mom would not have any problem with the decision.

Due to some DMV difficulties and a lack of understanding of registration procedures, my first car (the green 1950 Chevy that made me so popular at school) was never registered in my name or my parents' names. The reason for this was when I purchased the vehicle at the car lot, the owner was in the process of selling or trading it in for another one. Although we received all the proper paperwork for purchasing the vehicle, it happened that the person selling the car did not have the car paid off. When he received the cash, apparently, he did not pay the car off, which meant that the lean holder on the car was holding the pink slip or certificate of ownership. My parents didn't understand the legality of the situation for transferring ownership, so nothing was done. I wasn't going to pay the ninety-five dollars still owed. I also had no knowledge of the process.

Being very discouraged, I asked my dad to look for another car for me. Each car he would bring by the service station for me to see. After about four cars, he drove in with a 1955 Chevy two-door coupe. He could tell that I liked this one much better than the others that he had delivered. This Chevy had a lot of potential. However, while only making $1.50 an hour, I had to keep my focus on school, clothes, and expenses that a maturing male needs to have. Later, during my first year of junior college, a friend had a 1957 Chevy with a Corvette engine. He wanted to replace the current engine with one with more horsepower. It just so happened that I did also. I bought his 283 cubic inch; he bought the 327.

This only meant one thing. Paul a buddy of mine let me help him install the engine, and he hooked everything else up. This Corvette 283 bolted to the low-geared three-speed transmission that had been married to a six-cylinder engine meant the cruising of Main Street in Modesto was about to get better.

You have to know that in Modesto almost everyone cruised or raced on Tenth and Eleventh Streets during the mid-sixties. On occasion, the cruisers would get a glimpse of George Lucas, now a movie director of *American Graffiti*. As a side note, the street scenes in *American Graffiti* were actually done in Modesto. There seems to be someone who wants to cause trouble.

This was the case on Saturday night. Ron had a 1940 Ford four-door sedan with a red exterior and black interior. On this night, as we stopped for the line of cars in front of us, we were hit in the back by a nice 1959 Chevy Impala. The three guys got out, staggered over to us, and tried to blame Ron, saying the accident was his fault. He said the brake lights on Ron's 1940 Ford sedan were not working. As the police arrived, the officer checked out the brakes and found that the lights were, in fact, working. Needless to say, the three who were trying to start a fight with us that night got a free ride down to the jail, and the severely damaged Impala was hauled off.

We continued with our cruising down McHenry Avenue. One of the most exciting things about high school in Modesto and our weekend cruising on Tenth and Eleventh streets was the expansion of the cruise route of J Street and McHenry Avenue. Around eleven o'clock most of the hot rods and some of the cars that the owner thought were hot would be driven to a street on the west side of town that was marked off with quarter-mile strips. Just as in the movie *American Graffiti*, the quarter-mile street drag or race actually did occur in real time. George Lucas and the street racers actually did race their rods and rides.

Many times a fellow cruiser would cause a distraction of some sort and the police would chase the designated distractor down McHenry Boulevard or make a stop at Shakey's Pizza Parlor to break up a fight, which was usually a verbal and pushing altercation with no blood showing. During any chase or physical altercation for the distraction, the cars at the quarter-mile strip would pull up to the starting line, and in anxious anticipation, the drivers would rev up the engines (increase the rpm) and be ready for the white flag (a white T-shirt) to be dropped from the high-rise position down to right side of the person starting the race.

Of course, both sides of the quarter-mile strip were lined shoulder to shoulder with the onlookers cheering for the racers.

Some of the lookers didn't really care who would win the race. They were just hanging out with friends and peers only to be there. When the white flag came down and joined the right leg of the person starting the race, all the cheering and excitement levels were increased, and even the guys were jumping up and down.

As the cars came close to the end of the race strip, through the dim glow of the old streetlight and smoke, one could see the spectators involved in their own foot race as they tried to beat all the others to the end. The drivers would be laughing and talking about how one driver started the race with his bumper over the starting line or one car's engine coughed and hesitated at the beginning. It seemed the car that was the loser was driven by the guy with the excuses for being beat in the race by the other car and guide.

The trophy for the winner of each race was not a tall metal-and-wood symbol of victory but only a week of bragging rights that his or her car was the fastest or meanest for that week.

I finally graduated from Thomas Downey High School Modesto in 1964. I remember it being an end-to-end era for me. The graduation ceremony was held at the junior college campus on the lawn area. I was so proud that night. I was the third out of eight siblings to graduate from high school. The first was the oldest boy, Fred. The second was the youngest girl, Carol.

As the excitement began to build and the speakers began projecting the sound, I saw members of my family leaving. I knew it was very cool, and a slight breeze blew carrying the chill and helping the coolness that night. The excitement of the night quickly turned to discouragement. With an emptiness, I turned my heart and attention back to the ceremony when I suddenly noticed that I was not seated next to the person whom

I was supposed to be as I was during practice. I couldn't help to think, *I'll get someone else's diploma seated like this.*

It sure wasn't very long until I saw a lot of whispering going on. The other graduates also saw; something was wrong here. To this day, I don't know for sure how the seating order became so messed up and confusing. I bet I know why, however. The why question can only be answered by saying that some of the people graduating had not learned yet to listen or pay attention to instructions. Apparently, most everyone finally noticed that something was wrong.

As the ceremony continued, the visitors, family, and friends could clearly see something happened also. As the front row of graduates, in a slumped over position, began moving to the row in front of them. The second row did the same, the third row did the same, and it continued. Needless to say, every row moved to the row in front of them in this slumped-over position. The people in the audience began laughing as each graduate turned the corner on the end of the row in continued moving along the correct row. It was funny. Finally, it was over, but what I would give to return to those mishap days. Fortunately, we all received our diplomas the next day.

The summer after graduation I spent working just as my dad and grandparents had always done. I drove a tractor during the peach harvest and worked at the service station at night until ten o'clock. I would clean the drives and floors each night before closing, and the next day I'd do it again. I worked a lot because I had a car payment on a 1960 Chevy Impala two-door hardtop now, and I wanted to attend junior college in the fall of 1964) I wasn't sure exactly what I wanted to major in when going to college or what I wanted to do.

Like most unprepared and confused high school kids do, I was going to give college a try. I recall that my high school counselor told me that my scores on the aptitude test showed that my interest was very strong in the area of public service, so he recommended trying out the law-enforcement program at Modesto Junior College. If I didn't like it, I could always change. The option sounded good to me more so because my oldest brother, Fred, was a deputy sheriff in Los Angeles County in Southern California.

You should know at this point that there were actually three main reasons why I chose to go to junior college. The first, as I mentioned, was that I really didn't know what I wanted to do in life. The second was I wanted to be the first child of this migrant farm labor family to go to a college and finish. (A note here: Carol did attend one semester at Porterville Community College). The third reason was to avoid the draft.

Beginning college for me was quite scary. Because my sister Carol never talked to me about a life at college or what to do or what to expect, I entered into a new realism of life that no other family member had ever tried. I did major studies in the law-enforcement field. I was really excited and knew that this was my calling. About the middle of the first semester, Jack MacArthur, who was the departmental director at the time, called me into his office. I had no idea what this chat would be about.

My thoughts were on the possibility of conducting a special operations project or leading a law-enforcement team when we investigated a crime or something. The director sat me down at his desk and asked me about a felony hit-and-run accident that had shown up on my driving record, because a felony offense of anything would surely prevent me from continuing studies in his department.

Here is what I told him: The month after I had turned eighteen a friend and I went to a football friend's house to pick up his sister and her friend to go bowling. The car I was driving (the 1950 Chevy I mentioned earlier) had a short turning rod. As I backed in slowly to parallel park, the rear bumper hit a car, putting a small dent and scratch in the left-rear quarter panel near the left-rear tire. My friend Rod and I went inside Mack's house and told him what had happened. He said that the car belonged to his visiting uncle, and he just went out the front door. The three guys got into my car, and we went to the uncle's house and checked his favorite restaurant but did not find him.

Mack called him the next day and told him about the accident. During the next week after my classes and before going to work, I used my car and transported the uncle around town to look for a car for his daughter. The second week after the accident, a highway patrolman came out to my parents' trailer to look at my 1950 Chevy. The officer said that a hit-and-run complaint had been filed, and he was investigating the complaint. I told my dad about the incident. He advised me to go to court and plead guilty and pay the fine. Little did I know at that time that my dad knew almost less about the law than I did at the time. We went to court, and I entered the plea and was fined forty dollars for damages and four dollars for court costs.

Those were the facts of the case, and they were undisputed. Mr. McArthur told me that a hit-and-run meant that damage had been done to the property, and the guilty person left the scene. Because I did not leave the scene before the person who owned the vehicle did, I was not guilty of the hit-and-run charges. I was able to complete the law-enforcement program. The guilty plea and the advice of my dad has stayed on my driving record.

While I was attending junior college, it should be known

that a military conflict was going on in Southeast Asia, wherever that was. With this knowledge in the back of my mind, I knew that I had to be in and do well in school. Besides being involved with law-enforcement activities and security of the college campus, I wanted to be involved in something fun and relaxing. Because I had been involved in choir and men's glee club in high school and had fun participating in the musical productions and plays, like *Westside Story* and *Oklahoma*, I decided to join the concert choir at Modesto Junior College. To my surprise, also in the choir and in the concert band was the person whom I had missed for almost two years.

While a new high school (Grace Davis) was being constructed in Modesto, the students who were to attend the new school were attending Downey High School for about a year and a half. That is when I first met this mysterious gal. I can't remember exactly how the meeting happened, but afterward, we spent all of our free time in the student center together.

As the popular words are heard, love was in the air. The short relationship grew as we visited and talked with each other up to the day that the new high school was ready to receive its students. On that day, she was gone. Being naïve as I was, I didn't think to get any contact information from her at the time. I didn't even know her transfer and departure date, so there I was, alone and mildly heartbroken.

Sometime later, I met and became very close friends with Dorothy Steele. Our friendship was one of brother and sister. You'll read more about her and how she changed and improved my life later. For about two and a half years, until I graduated from high school, I thought about the phantom girl and wondered if I would see her during our graffiti cruises or someplace else or ever. So there was the phantom gal, or at least

I thought it was her, walking down the corridor of the music building at the community college.

After two or three days of passing her each day, I finally found the courage to ask her if she was the girl who had attended Thomas Downey High School and transferred. To my relief, it was her, and she was not dating anyone. Lucky for me. Evelyn and I started dating when we could. I had a full-time school schedule and still worked at the service station seven days a week. The station had a name change when Phillips 66 Oil Company purchased Associated (Flying A) Oil Company.

I will never forget one weekend when my older brother Fred, who was a deputy sheriff in Los Angeles County, brought his family up to Empire to visit the family. This was November or December 1964. He had sold his 1957 Corvette, which he'd had the last time I'd seen him, and bought a black-on-black 1963 Corvette. What a good brother. He picked me up after work at the station, and we went for a cruise in his brand-new Corvette. What a thrill this ride was for me. Not only was I with my big brother, whom I respected and looked up to, but we were in a new body-style Corvette cruising town.

That cruise in that Corvette locked in for me the passion that I have for the Corvette. But I knew that I would have to wait for mine. Upon the return of the college choir and band from a competition concert in Long Beach, California, I found that Evelyn became pregnant while at the competition. So though somewhat brokenhearted, because my parents had taught about the importance of family, I discontinued my relationship with my mystery girl.

She did have a beautiful baby girl a few months later. She did bring the baby by one day while I was at work.

During the last year or year and a half of my experience at Modesto Junior College, I was bombarded with notices from the selective service board in Modesto. The military had activated the draft each of the three or four times that I had received mine. I had to return, stating that I was still attending college. After three years at Modesto Junior College, it came time to attempt graduating. So in June 1967, I again participated in a graduation ceremony that none of my family and a very few friends came to. Although I was somewhat disappointed, I knew that I was the seventh child and the first to complete college courses and graduate. Oh well, such is life. I am not sure why my family did not attend any of my graduation ceremonies. The only conclusions that I can come up with are that they either did not understand the importance of the accomplishment and the feeling that came with it or they worried about the cool weather that came along with the cooling of the evening.

After graduation, I did receive a draft notice to leave for military services on January 4, 1968. For the summer and fall of 1967, I continued working late afternoons at the service station and worked the graveyard shift at the Modesto plant of Campbell's Soup Company loading and unloading railcars of merchandise and products. To my dismay, not much happened after graduating until the date of my departure to the military.

Before I proceed much further, I had better mentioned an important fact for the interest and awareness of the younger readers to set the stage for a better understanding of the feeling and concerns of the 1960s era, which resulted in some very important development and decisions that affected all of our lives today. The era of the 1960s was a very trying and troubled time for our country. It seemed to be a time of growth that nobody was prepared for. From this unsuspected growth spurt came many changes and new arrival of things that people didn't understand or couldn't explain.

The 1960s was, or at least seemed to be, an era of drugs, sex, and rock and roll. First of all, the use of drugs came out of the closet, so to speak. The various drugs were smoked, injected, or ingested out in the open and in public view. Sexual promiscuity became rampant and also out in the open. The use of drugs caused disillusionment, as the users were high most of the time. Their self-indulging became more important to them. Because I was continuously working and had plans for a future, I was able to refrain from becoming involved in the movement of the sixties. However, I did have a few friends who did. Some lost their lives because of their use of the drugs.

The rock and roll music element also played a major role by using lyrics that were more suggestive and filled the drug user and abuser brain with thoughts and images in areas that the drug of choice missed. Frequently, I was approached and offered any variety of drugs, even while I was at work. I always refused, because I had no reason to indulge. To give an example of what was happening and how people were affected by the drug use and becoming high to have the "free" and "loose" feelings, I would only now to mention Woodstock, which took place in an open field in New York State, and the Monterey Pop Festival, which was in the central coast town of Monterey, California. From these festivals came some of my favorite music, although I was not involved in the movement.

Both of these music events had great music and many artist involved in the aftermath. Most people have heard of tie-dyed shirts, make love not war, baggy pants, long hair, flowers in your hair, the flower children, flower child, and the VW bus painted with psychedelic colors. Guess where they got their beginning.

The Haight-Ashbury district in San Francisco also became a very popular place to be. Another advancement was the visual coverage of daily events outside of US borders by TV and reporters. The main concern seemed to be the Vietnam conflict. All of these things contributed to the negative sentiments that were laced upon the veterans as we returned after our tours of duty. Just thought people might want to know.

Chapter 6

The morning of January 4, 1968, came very early. Because I was awake and up most of the night in anticipation of what was to come anyway, that morning seemed to be a continuation of the night before. I had my articles packed that were on the list provided by Selective Service Board 55. The instructions given on paper were as follows: you are to be at the Stanislaus County Library on I Street (near Eleventh Street) on the morning of January 4, 1968, at four o'clock in the morning for transportation pickup. I didn't think at the time it would be a good idea to have my older parents get out of bed at three o'clock in the morning in order to take me to the place of rendezvous that time of morning. After all, they were up in the years. I think my dad was sixty-seven, and my mom was sixty-one.

However, my thoughts were not warranted. Now that I am past their age at that date, I can clearly see how important it would have been to them to be able to spend the last hour or so with their son leaving for the military. I assumed that it probably wouldn't be really that significant of a send-off. My older brother Fred had been in the US Air Force for four years, and I doubted that they'd seen him off when he enlisted.

As a matter of fact, I recall only seen him one time during his long four-year hitch, and that was just before I graduated from basic training at Parks Air Force base in Alameda County (east bay area). My parents had to ask directions all the way to the barracks he was in. It must have been on a Sunday. We saw him walking down the street. He stopped to talk about five or ten minutes, and then he was off again. I'm sure that my parents were disappointed after driving two hours from Modesto and only talking for a short time.

None of our family attended his graduations from high school, basic training, or his tech school. Remembering this disappointment that my parents had to experience visiting my brother, I didn't want to witness or have them experience that feeling again as I was leaving. I was sure wrong assuming. I did hear about it later. My girlfriend at the time met me at our home, and after hugs and kisses and words of wisdom, we were off.

Because my dad was too young for the military service during World War I and somewhat too old with too many mouths to feed during World War II, he didn't get to experience the military service part of life, which included the initial departure of a son who would be going overseas.

As we arrived at the I Street county library building in Modesto, I saw ten or twelve guys waiting for the ride. After unloading my one small piece of luggage (a brown grocery-type bag), I saw a couple of guys I knew from Modesto Junior College. I had no idea that I would have company or know anyone who would be taking the long ride with me. I arrived at the requested location at 3:50 a.m. It was a good thing I was a little early. The bus that was going to do the honors arrived precisely at 3:45 a.m. for the 4:00 departure. There was sure no room for error, like being late.

By 4:15 a.m., we were on our way going south on the Highway 99, which is the main traveling artery in California's

Central Valley. I recall the bus stopped in Turlock, Merced, Chowchilla, and Madera. At each of these towns we were joined by five to ten more recruits. Our final stop on the slate of our long journey was Fresno. The education center of Fresno—what a place it was.

As we each stepped off the transporter, we were taken into a large, open room. Our luggage and bags were checked to make sure that the items on the instruction sheet were all accounted for. We each had to strip down to our boxers, briefs, or whatever, and we all had very high hopes that every guy had something on after removing his outer pants. Using a line-production system, we were all given the turn-your-head-and-cough exam. Our throats, glands, and breathing were also all checked.

The proctors (all military personnel) each had a particular function to perform to make the line production proceed. After the swearing into the military service, one of the proctors told us to remember the branch of service that he told each of us as we walked down the line of inductees still standing in their briefs and boxers. As he walked, he stopped momentarily and would call off a branch of the service. There were very few chosen for the coast guard, and a few chosen for the navy. The majority of the group were chosen for the Army and the Marines. Our next process was the paperwork. The Coast Guard's men were taken to the Guard's cubicle. The Navy men were taken to their cubicle, the Army people were taken to a small room, and the Marines people were taken to another room. I was shuffled into the Army area.

In these rooms, we were given a very short explanation of military life and what would be expected. All the induction papers were agreed to and signed. Our delicious lunch was a sandwich and a cup of water or tea. This induction process took until about three or four o'clock that afternoon. When everyone was processed, we boarded a bus and were taken to the Fresno air terminal for the next leg in our adventure. During our hour and a half (our first experience with hurry up and wait) delay, all of us receive our serial or ID number. This number would be on our dog tags and every piece of paper that was related to us. My serial number was US56669844. We were to have our numbers memorized before we boarded the plane that would take us into the wild blue yonder to our next destination.

Finally, we were allowed to get on board. There were no assigned seats, so we could sit in any seat. There just so happened to be a military personnel directing us to seats as we entered. As row A was full, he moved back to row B. When row B was full, next came row C, and then row D, and so on. I figured he was there to see that all the seats were filled and done in a timely manner. As the last inductee was seated and secured in his seat, I could hear the first engine begin to whine.

As the rpm began to increase, the whine changed into a low rumble as the six blades of the propeller turned faster in preparation for takeoff. Not a minute passed before the second whine began, and the same sound of the rumble filled my ears. The third engine whined and rumbled, and it also smoothed as it followed suit of the first and second ones. About thirty seconds after the third engine began its humming, the fourth started its whine and rumbled, and all four engines began humming in harmony like a well-trained concert symphony. As soon as the symphony of the engines were well into their performance piece, the plane began to move toward the runway of the air terminal. Because we were the only plane on the runway and the four prop engines were humming their song, we began to move down the long runway in the northwest direction.

Although it seemed as if we had only traveled about a semi-truck's length, the front of the vessel began to lift up while the rear tires were still rolling on the asphalt of the runway. The next event was unbelievable. About a minute later, it was as if we were floating in midair. This day was the first time I had ever flown and experienced such a thrill. As the four prop engines concerted together, the plane climbed higher and higher to an altitude permissible for cruising and out of the path of other possible air traffic. Then off we went.

Recently, I flew on a twin-engine prop plane from Fresno to Seattle for my grandson's high school graduation. This flight was a two-hour air cruise, so I'm guessing that the flight in 1968 on a four-engine prop plane took the same two hours. That guess would take into consideration the advancement in technology, both mechanical and fuel. While the four engines were humming their song in 1968, many thoughts raced through my mind. With this flight being my maiden ride and seeming to be floating in air while listening to the humming, believe me many things did pop up in my mind.

The first thing that popped up was the hope that the humming did not stop. The stopping would not be a good thing in a lot of ways. Another thing was that I wondered what I was getting myself into. Maybe I should have joined Bill and the other guys who chose to go to Canada. (Many young men chose to go to Canada in order to avoid being drafted into the military.) I sure didn't know what I would do or where I would go in Canada.

Throughout each generation in my family going all the way back to the early 1800s, the men did not wimp out. Each man faced and dealt with what he faced each day. I guess going into the military and not knowing what to expect was my "facing it." This journey that I was embarking on was the first time ever for me to be away from the comforts of home that my parents had struggled so long and hard to provide for me, as well as all seven of my siblings.

I found myself wondering how my parents could be accepting of my leaving and if they'd be okay as they worried about me. I also realized that I would miss the life I had always known and miss the way things were. Things were about to change forever.

Somehow the pilot was able to find the Sea-Tac (Seattle-Tacoma) Airport through the darkness of the night. I am sure glad that the continuous humming did not put him to sleep. Of course, the way the military did things for you becoming a new member of the family was to travel at night. So that is what we did upon our safe arrival in Seattle. All of the inductees were counted as we stepped on to what looked like the same bus we'd been on in Fresno.

Remember I said that each recruit had to memorize the number that was given him while waiting at the Fresno air terminal? Well, guess what. We were all required to recite the long number before being allowed to board the bus. It looked as though everyone had done what he was told. We all boarded and hoped that the driver knew where he was going as the bus split through and broke the silence as it went rambling down the no-see zone. The dark bus trip must have taken about an hour from Sea-Tac to the area where we would actually begin our lives as US Army recruits.

Our first stop was the gates of Fort Lewis Washington Military Compound. Passing through the gates that were visible under the illumination of the night security lights, the bus continued rolling on toward our second and final stop for the night. Our final stop happened to be the new-recruit receiving station. As we stepped off the night bus, we were immediately taken into a large warehouse-type building. This building contained all the GI (government-issued) items that we had to have. These items, unknown to us, were going to be a large part of life-changing experiences. We received our fatigue (OD green work clothes), T-shirts, OD green socks, a helmet and helmet liner, a belt with a buckle, and our OD green bedding supplies. We were then given a duffel bag to put the GI clothes in when traveling. Guess what color.

After each new recruit received all the issued items, we carried our gifts toward a two-story building that would be our home for an unknown number of weeks. As we entered the two-story house, we were assigned a first or second floor. As I entered onto the second floor, I saw two long rows of bunk beds with no bedding. Bewildered, I now knew why we had been given the blankets and sheets. After receiving our assigned bunks, we each went to the assignment and unloaded the GI items onto the bed. Thank God my bunk was on the bottom.

Each of us had to spread the sheets out and make up his bed to get ready for the long-deserved rest. It was then that I actually realized and appreciated what my mom taught years before about how to make a bed. As each relaxed on his own GI bed and began to get acquainted better with other recruits, none of us even looked at or paid any attention to the floor. The next morning we were awaken as early as we had to be to meet the bus in Modesto. It was then that we noticed how clean and spit-shined the floor was (which you will read more about in a later chapter).

After our first military shave, we had to line up in sort of a formation. After some instructions had been given, we were escorted to breakfast. The first row of the formation was seated at the first table. The second row at the second table and so on. After going through the chow line and getting our metal sectioned plate filled, we sat down. While eating, we continued on our conversations from the night before. About ten minutes after we sat down, our military overseer came over and told us that chow was over. In a loosely fitted formation, we walked back to our new home the barracks.

During the instructional formation, we learned how to salute, who to salute, and when to salute. We learned and practiced the art of standing at attention and the command for that. After those were mastered, the instructor (drill corporal) asked if anyone had gone to college. A few of us had attended. Those who had gone to college and graduated were placed in leadership positions. I became fourth squad leader. A side note, a squad consisted of ten to twelve people, and four squads comprised a platoon.

From that first day, we were taught how to march. We marched as a group (platoon) and learned all of the commands to partner with marching. When the noon chow time came, we formed up into our squads and platoons, and off we marched to the mess hall. Each squad was seated at their table. It was funny; no one said anything at this meal. It was the first of many silent meals that were to come. After lunch, we were taught how to make a tight bed and how to military fold our socks, boxers, and T-shirts. The placement in our assigned footlockers (a military trunk) for these items was very critical and had to be organized in such a way to be pleasing to the inspecting officer when and if an unexpected inspection was called.

Our fatigues (work uniforms) had to be hung in the closet with care, and all the hangers had to be hung so that the metal hook was facing toward the back of the closet. The dress shoes, as well as the GI boots, had to be kept in a spit-shine condition, as did the belt buckles. After learning these few basic things about the military, I was ready to move on to the next phase.

We were at the new-recruit receiving station for two weeks. Many times while I was at this receiving station I wondered why the military would send me all the way from almost the middle of the state of California to the state of Washington in the middle of the winter when I could have been sent to Fort Ord Army Training Base near Monterey, California, for the same training.

As I later found out, the military does a lot of things that would be very hard to explain. When our two weeks at the receiving station were completed, the entire group was loaded on a bus that looked like the one in Modesto two weeks earlier, and we were transported to our basic training on the North Fort section of Fort Lewis Army Base. At North Fort, my group was taken to its training area and was joined with another small group to form a company of two platoons (usually a company has four platoons); this union of the two groups became C Company.

The basic training companies at Fort Lewis were closed companies, which meant that no recruit could leave or go out of the company area. When the company area was going to be left behind, we had to leave in a formation, and the entire two platoons had to go. (A side note: this restriction should be kept in mind. It will come up again later.)

As things go, we began basic training. Keep in mind as you read that C Company came together and began twelve or so weeks of training in the middle of winter and in the middle of snow and mud. Fort Lewis, Washington, is at the south end of Puget Sound and at that time received about twelve to fifteen inches of snow every winter.

I was sure surprised and shocked because I had come from a drier and much-warmer California. Each person who was selected as a squad leader at the receiving station prior to North Fort retained the position throughout the training cycle. Being a leader of a squad or platoon had its advantages. We were allowed to avoid extra duties, such as kitchen patrol (aka KP) and cleaning offices and the day room. So having the responsibilities of a leader did come with advantages.

The twelve weeks of training were vigorous. Having to march through the snow and mud did not help at all. Every morning after shaving in getting ready for the day and before we were allowed to see the inside of the mess hall, we had to run as a company group. At the beginning of the training cycle, the distance was about two miles. By the end of training, we were running six or seven miles. After our morning run, we went to breakfast. After eating, we "saddled up" (put on our pack and gear) and went off to train.

The training consisted of a section on weapons disassembling and reassembling, cleaning and care, and firing at the various prepared ranges. Classroom education was also a big part of what we learned. After each day of training, we would be taken to other various activities, such as getting the multiple shots, having dental checkups and visual exams, and, oh yes, receiving a haircut every week.

Although I was never fortunate enough to have an opportunity to go to summer camp when I was younger—or play the games I would hear about each fall, when my friends would return from their summer vacations—somehow I was able equate my experiences during my military training to the fun and games I participated in during my everyday life as if I had been at summer camp. I was able to make my physical training and the endurance training course into a game-like situation, which allowed me to be able to have fun and strive harder at each event.

This was true during PT (physical training) time in the

snow. Fort Lewis is adjacent to McChord Air Force Base. In 1968, the air force was flying cargo transport missions using C-141s. The C-141 is a huge four-jet engine aircraft with a very high rear tail and a wingspan so long that when the aircraft is on the ground, the wings shag down so the tip of each wing is close to the ground. It sure didn't matter what PT exercise we were doing; we could look up out of the snow and mud to watch these planes make their approach to land. The four huge fan jet engines would whine as the air was passing through the fan inside the engine housing. I was able to adjust my cadence while doing PT to coincide with the rhythm of the concert sound of the mighty engines as they worked to lower the weight they were carrying closer and closer to the ground.

Besides, to watch this massive bird pass near us was amazing. The sight of such a machine and the recalling in my memory of its flight helped me to sustain my endurance and successfully complete each obstacle, and with it, my PT objectives seemed to take less effort. At the very least, I was able to keep my mind off the unpleasant journey and change the unpleasant task to a more enjoyable one.

During our Sunday off, we were allowed to go to a movie. I can't remember whose idea it was, but it seemed that everyone wanted to go do something. So we got into the squad/platoon formation and marched down to see a movie called *The Good, the Bad and Ugly*, which was one of Clint Eastwood's B movies. I was good to relax and get my mind off of training.

One Sunday it was fourth squad's turn to clean the offices and day room. Most of the recruits on my squad were cooperative and would help. As you know, there is always one who refuses. That probably was from having everything done for him before the military. So it was that fourth squad had one of those too. Another situation where the uncooperative recruit was not helping our labors and efforts was on a Sunday when our platoon was given permission to make a phone call home. Some of the guys did not choose to call.

The men who wanted to take turns using the single phone booth in our company area were assigned a specific allotted time. Guess who would be in charge. While each person was making his ten-minute call, it seemed that the same spoiled brat began trying to rush each caller so he would have more time to talk when his turn came. Needless to say, his turn did not come that time around.

As the training cycle continued, the weapons training became more interesting, despite the cold snow. For one training, we were transported by truck to near the lower end of Mount Reiner to a special weapons range. During this operation, a sergeant noticed that one trainee from the second squad seemed to have a five o'clock shadow at nine o'clock in the morning. When questioned, the trainee responded by telling the range training sergeant that he had shaved the night before to avoid the early morning rush. Remember earlier when I said that there were certain items that we had to carry in our packs that were on the list sent by the selective service board? Well, a double-edged razor and a new blade were two of the required items.

On this training day, the sergeant had a guy take the razor and blade out of his pack and shave. The guy was going to use water from his belt canteen to wet his face so what he was going to have to do would be a little less abrasive. To his dismay, he was not able to use any moisture and had to dry shave in order to remove the shadow and let the brighter face shine. As time passed by, I began to learn why we were instructed to carry various items in our pack. Our temporary encampment in the open, also known as *Bivouac* (French), was a time when everyone seemed to not look forward to.

Most of the trainees thought of this as the navy SEAL's hell week when the training SEALs stayed wet and cold for one week and were required to do various operations as a team and work together. We were told what we going to be doing during this exercise and what we needed to take for personal supplies. The Sunday before we were to leave we marched to the Post Exchange (PX) to purchase the supplies that we needed. The one item that we were told not to bring was Sterno. (To be informed, Sterno is a solid, alcohol-based product in a can that can be used for heating or cooking when a person goes camping.) The flame that emits from the solidified alcohol burns blue and cannot be seen for a distance in the dark. Because there was snow on the ground and the cold of the night would be engulfing us with an attempt to chill us to the bone, we had to do something to avoid being cold all night.

Needless to say, the shelves were empty of Sterno when we left the PX store. I believe that we were told not to get the Sterno by our training staff even though they knew we would be more likely to bring it anyway. Even though I did take my Sterno also, this campout was somewhat like that trip that my buddies in high school took overnight to a local lake east of Modesto. At the lake outing, we did not have anything to keep us warm as we slept on the beach area and the freezing wind washed over us all night. This campout would be very close to the same.

The difference for me this time was the Sterno to keep warm and out of sight. On this military temporary encampment, each of us had a very unusual bed partner. I'm sure everyone's was the same, but mine was cold, lumpy, and hard. It only moved when I moved and did not talk at all. My M-14 carbine training rifle only spoke on the rifle range.

During the day, we went on maneuvers in groups of three one day, four different guys the next day, and the entire squad the third day. Each group was given an assignment to accomplish. For me, the outing was a fun adventure and exciting experience. We were trucked back to the company area and were able to warm up that night.

Previously I made mention of the incident about company area restrictions. So here is the story behind that. About three weeks before we were finished with the twelve weeks of training I knew that Valentine's Day was getting close. I also knew and had been in close touch with a high school friend who I became close to before I graduated. We had and still have a brother/sister relationship.

Dorothy was a sergeant in the Air Force and just happened to be stationed at McChord Air Force Base. As Valentine's Day was approaching, Dottie decided to take a seven-day leave and return to Modesto. During one phone call to her, she let me know about the leave she was taking. I asked her if she would be willing to deliver a box of candy and a couple of cards if I purchased them. The candy was for my then girlfriend, and one card was for my mother. She agreed to meet me on the side road nearest to C Company.

This meant I would have to cross through D Company's area to get to the road. With the time and location set, I purchased the candy and card at PX. Under the cover of darkness, I gathered my items, and upon entering D Company's boundary, I began sneaking from one building to a bush to another building and then to a hedge. With security in mind and very cautiously, I and my path across unknown territory until I spotted Dottie's VW bug sitting in the darkness.

I greeted my sister/friend and gave her the Valentine items. She waited until I began my return before she started her VW and drove off. I knew that Dottie was dependable, and of all people I knew, I could count on her. The items did reach their destinations. As for me, as I returned instead of building to bush to building and so on, I chose a different route. I knew the package had been delivered, and I didn't see anyone as I crossed the unknown territory. Because I felt so confident, I felt like walking across the D Company area to return.

As I approached the halfway point of my return journey, I entered the open area that D Company used to conduct their formations and drills. And who should I just happened to meet there? It was D Company's CQ (charge of quarters). He must not have recognized me as a D Company family member. Being reared by my parents to face the consequences to situations as the hit-and-run case, I admitted that my family was C Company. He told me to go and report to the C Company CQ. It sure crossed my mind whether to report. I choose to report.

The CQ seemed to take the violation of the company rules quite well. He told me to go to bed and we would talk about it the next day. I wasn't sure if I should have dreaded the next day. From the tone of his voice, all would be good, so I didn't think much more about the subject. The next morning came, and I got ready for the day's training, ate breakfast, and waited for my squad to form up.

After all four squads were in formation, our company CXO (company executive officer) came out to our platoon. We all snapped to attention. He walked over to fourth squad and told everyone to parade rest except me. I had to remain in the stance of attention. I figured this was the talk that the CQ had talked about. The second lieutenant began chewing me on the left side and then chewed up to the top of my head and all the way down the right side of my feet. Of course, I did deserve the talk, but I was embarrassed to be talked to in such a tone in front of my squad. I knew the lieutenant did the talk as he did in order to use my situation as an example to the other men. Up to that point, I thought he was a very cool leader. He was fresh out of OCS (officers candidate school), and more importantly, he drove a new 1968 Corvette.

Approximately two or three weeks after the D Company incident it was time for graduation. I assume that the basic trainees completed the military requirements, or this cadre was tired of us whining. Our entire company (both platoons) spent most of one day practicing our marching, cadence, and training. The evening before the ceremony I called my adopted sister Dottie to confirm that she and Peggy were still going to come to see the miracle of basic graduation. After receiving her confirmation, I had a feeling of excitement, like I had really accomplished something vital. And a sister would be there to share it all with me.

Graduation day came. Each trainee was spit-shined and had fresh, heavily starched fatigues on. We were transported in that familiar bus that I thought was in Modesto. As each company from our battalion arrived, it took its place on the paradise field. As C Company arrived, I looked to see if Dottie and Peggy had arrived. I did not see any familiar faces in the crowd of about 150 parents and relatives.

As we began marching, I sneaked a few glimpses at the bleachers to see if the familiar faces were there. After the marching and the speeches, the two platoons of our company were transported back to the company area. We were given the afternoon off. While I was roaming the company area and wondering if I would ever miss it, guess who drove up in the light-blue VW bug. She said that she got busy finishing a project so she could come by and pick me up to run around. (I took that to mean cruising.)

As Dottie stepped out of the bug and the company cadre and some of the trainees saw the stripes on her uniform (which indicated rank and time in service), I saw a lot of jaws drop in disbelief. Even the lieutenant who was standing on the step of the company's office took a second look. As I walked toward the freedom machine to meet her, I just had to throw my chest out a little farther and show my pride that a fellow military person was going to run off with me for a couple of hours.

The night after our graduation would be our last at C Company. The following morning we had instructions to roll our bedding up and turn it in to laundry services. During the hours that passed that new day, each of the basic graduates received his orders for the next duty station. The men of both platoons were scattered across the country to the advanced training base for the field/job for which he enlisted.

For those of us who were drafted, there wasn't much of a choice. I remember a few of the guys went to Texas, a couple to Kansas, and some to Kentucky and Georgia. A few even stayed at Fort Lewis to receive further training. However, Dennis of Iowa and I both went to Fort Polk, Louisiana. During our basic training, I happened to be in the First Platoon, and Dennis was in the Second Platoon. Being in the same basic training company, I knew who he was, but we never became friends until we received our orders to the sweat box of the South.

As we said our farewells to the others we'd spent twelve weeks eating and sleeping with, I realized I would never see any of them again. I flashed back in my pea brain to a Sunday during our training cycle when I volunteered to assist at the visitors' center on post. Of course, this volunteer assignment occurred on the same day that the C Company squad picture was being taken.

After I arrived at the center, I was told just to look and walk around and see if any civilian visitors needed help of any kind. I was going to enjoy this challenge. About thirty minutes into this assignment, I happened to notice an elderly woman who seemed to be lost or looking for someone. I approached her and asked if she needed any help. She said she was waiting for her grandson who was supposed to meet her. I set her at a table and got her a glass of juice. I was going to visit with her until her grandson arrived. The grandson never showed up, so I spent the remaining time sharing stories with her and learning about her relationship with her grandson. I regret not getting to know her more. She had some great stories to share, and I hope that her grandson took the small amount of time to really know her and listen to the stories of her family that she had to tell.

I had to bid her farewell and wished her luck during her next attempt. Getting my thoughts back on track, Dennis and I gathered our belongings in the duffle bag and took a familiar bus to Seattle-Tacoma Airport for the next leg of our long journey in the Army.

I am not sure if the flight to Fort Polk was a military or civilian flight, and I am not sure exactly where the flight landed. Remember I mentioned that night flying was the order of the day. Our flight almost had to end in or near Alexandria, Louisiana, because I do remember that infamous familiar-looking bus splitting through the black of night with only the headlight giving us a direction of travel. Dennis and I both tried to take advantage of the dark and put out our nets to catch some sleep.

On this famous-looking bus were recruits who had also completed their basic training at various forts around the country and were anxious to get to Fort Polk for advance training. As a side note, Pres. Dwight Eisenhower, a four-star general, completed his infantry training at Fort Polk. That was good to know. As the infamous bus pulled into the company compound and stopped, the yelling by the sergeants started immediately. All of the passengers were told to get into formation. *Why in the heck are they yelling?* I wondered.

They counted the men standing at attention—one, two, one, two—as they walked through formation until they had no more men to count. The ones would go to the barracks to the right. The twos would go to the housing on the left. Because Dennis and I were standing next to each other, I became a one and he became a two, which meant that we would not be in the same barracks together as we had hoped.

Well here we were at another training cycle. The temperatures were going to be on the exact opposite end of the temperature scale than they were at Fort Lewis, Washington; I acknowledged this the first day. I doubted the training would be as nice either. For me, AIT (Advanced Infantry Training) at Fort Polk North Fort was going to be similar to my basic training. After shaving, showering, and getting ready for each training day and before chow time, guess what we got to do. We ran five miles while in formation.

The big difference at Fort Polk was that we were able to run in our T-shirts. Another *big* difference was we were given a day and a half off each week, I would guess, because of the depth and intensity of the advanced training. We seemed to fast jog as a two-platoon company almost everywhere we went. The jog was in full pack and weapons. Some of the physical agility training was the same kind of course that the Army Airborne Rangers trained on. The intensity of the training was what made each weekend something to look forward to.

Some of the guys would take the opportunity leave post and go into Leesville, which was the nearby town. Other guys would have relatives come for the weekend. Such was the case with Dennis and me when the weekend arrived.

Dennis's dad worked in construction and happened to be working in the area between Shreveport and Alexandria on Highway 49. When Dennis and his dad began planning weeks before, Dennis and I went to the PX (Post Exchange) and purchased our civilian clothes. This attire was Levi's, a shirt, and a light pair of Hush Puppies shoes. We wore them a few times before Dennis's dad was to arrive.

The arrival weekend came finally. Dennis made arrangements. His dad was going to pick us up at noon on Saturday, and we would be off into the sunset. Well, guess what. When we were finished at noon with the training for the day, I was put on a detail (extra assignment) for a couple of hours. Dennis's dad was gracious enough to agree to return when my detail was finished.

It wasn't soon enough, but we were finally off. To this day, I am not sure exactly where we went or where we ended up except we did stay in a good motel for Saturday night. We traveled and enjoyed the scenic countryside on Sunday after breakfast. Every trainee who left the post and company for a weekend had to be back at the company by six o'clock in the evening to allow time for some to sober up and others to prepare for Monday's training. That weekend was the only one that Dennis and I left post.

Other weekends were spent touring the post and enjoying the weekend freedom. During the twelve weeks of AIT, I stayed in touch with everyone at home with more emphasis on touching the girl left behind. Being about 1,600 miles away from Modesto did create some difficulty. We had planned on getting married when I returned home. While I was at Fort Polk, she planned a small wedding and invited a few friends and relatives. The venue was set. She was excited for me to be home on a leave.

As at Fort Lewis, upon completing our training assignment, we completed the graduation ceremony process and returned to our Fort Polk company home. The next morning each of us packed up our personal things, placed them into our GI duffel bags, and rolled up our GI bedding as prescribed. After breakfast, we were formed up (into formation) and got ready to receive orders for either duty station or going home on a short leave. Each of the guys in both platoons received their orders when his name was called. There were four recruits out of the two entire platoons whose names were called last.

Guess who one of them was. The last four called gathered closer as all the other names were leaving the area to find out where we were going. My name was called, and I received an assignment for TDY (temporary duty) for eight weeks to Fort Knox, Kentucky. I was going to APC (armored personnel carrier) school. I immediately thought about my fiancée and how she was not going to like this news.

We were to leave the following day for Kentucky. That afternoon I called her to let her know that I wouldn't be coming home for eight more weeks. A person can only imagine what went on after receiving that news. Trying to avoid changing the entire plans for the wedding and notifying all of the invited guest of the unexpected postponement, she made suggestions like, "Tell the army that you are coming home to get married; tell them that you can't go Kentucky. Don't you love me anymore?" I spent what seemed to be an hour on the phone attempting to explain to her that I belonged to the military, and I had to do what they ordered when they ordered it.

Although she had a total lack of understanding of many things in life, which included military things, she finally conceded that there was nothing we could do about our situation. Later that afternoon we were once again loaded on to the infamous military bus and left behind our twelve weeks of severe training, which would probably be the most beneficial education, fitness, and preparedness for what was to come.

Once again, the engines of the aircraft spoke in harmony as they each worked to thrust the big bird into the evening sky. When we arrived in Kentucky, another bus was waiting to take us to our new company at Fort Knox. Our assignment while at Fort Knox for the eight weeks was APC school. An APC (armored personnel carrier) is a diesel-powered armored vehicle that will transport supplies and personnel anywhere. Although it is very slow and travels on a rotating track (as a military tank), it can actually travel and swim in the water. This eight-week temp duty was very different and easy compared to the past two training cycles that we had endured.

This cycle of training with school and related training went from eight o'clock in the morning to noon, then we had an hour for a great hot meal, and then we went again from one o'clock until five o'clock in the evening. We had every weekend off to do whatever. One of the days of the training we had to sacrifice and spend most of the day at the mess hall kitchen. Our duty there was to cut the eyes and skins off the russet potatoes.

The hands-on part of our APC training was to night drive and take the unit for a swim. Driving in a column at night requires each unit operator to keep a visual on the very small, almost-closed-eye taillight of the unit ahead. If the taillight could not be seen, the operator had to increase the speed of his unit until the red of the almost-closed eye could be seen. If the red of the taillight was too bright, the speed had to be decreased. This is similar to driving a vehicle on today's highways.

The most fun part of driving the machine came when we were allowed to drive into the water of the nearby training lake. Of course, with the machine's weight being in the range of two tons or more and doubting if all this weight would actually swim, I wondered if part of the training would be getting out of the tank and making sure that everyone got out alive. As the small dinosaur tank entered the cold water, to my surprise and I am sure to everyone's, we actually began to float.

We were instructed to increase pressure on the accelerator. When I did, the unit began to seemingly swim. As we swam across the lake, I saw a small hill that seemed to be my way of getting out of the water. The instructor told me that the hill had to be climbed. I told him, "Yeah right." In the classroom, the climbing of a wet and muddy hill must have been covered on one of the days. As the carrier began to roll out of the mud and water of the lake, I did have my doubts.

Following instructions as I heard the training officer yell them, I allowed the tracks of the carrier to dig into the soft mud and move it aside to find the solidness of the mound. The tracks gripped onto it to roll us out of the wetness of the lake. What a thrill that ride was. Returning to the garage, we repeated the procedure of following the small red taillights, the same as we'd done driving to the lake.

All went well, and we parked the carriers and turned off the hot diesel engines. This experience was talked about for a day or two afterward by all. After the eight weeks of this assignment, each of us was allowed to go home for two weeks before heading for our most dreaded next assignment. The two weeks I was home on leave was a whirlwind time.

Not only did my fiancée want all of my time, but some of

my relatives wanted some time to catch up. Then came the few true friends who wanted a visit too. One of the things that has really meant a lot to me came from a Korean veteran named Jay who had returned from Korea a wounded veteran. He lived in the labor camp in Empire where I lived while in high school and junior college. I knew that once a month he received a government check, but I didn't know what it was for. I knew he had a drinking problem. Every month after the first he would get a disability check. He was always a loner and never talked to anyone or told anyone about himself.

The morning that I arrived at my parents' mobile home at about five o'clock in the morning, I had to wake everyone out of their slumber. After the hugs and greetings from my mom, my dad finally made an appearance. To my surprise, he also greeted me with a hug and a smile. Being too anxious and excited about being home, being in the Army, and seeing everyone, I chose to iron my khaki uniform. Of course, my mom, being a mom and seeing her son iron his clothes, did offer to iron them while I sat and visited. Not only did my mom not know how to iron military creases, but I was now an American soldier and could do it myself.

Of course, I did not dare to tell her that. As I folded the areas of the shirt to be pressed, I began telling my inquisitive parents how the Army had made me army strong and what had been going on. After spit-shining my brand-new black dress shoes, I also pressed the traveling wrinkles out of the pants. When I was finished with my soldier chore and had made my parents confident that I was all right, I carefully stepped into the freshly ironed pants and shirt. The shirt proudly displayed one yellow chevron on each sleeve and a national defense ribbon on my upper-left chest. As I stepped out of the trailer to meet the camp world, I had to hesitate a moment to reflect back on the days when I ruled the half-dirt/half-asphalt roads and rolled the old tires with my friends. With my brass shining bright, I stepped down onto the dirty yard and began walking.

Now, I wasn't actually sure where I was going to walk to, but I knew that I didn't have to run this time. As I walked down the road that went next to Jay's parents' round-top, corrugated metal bungalow, I saw Jay walking out as if coming to meet me. That may not have been his intention, but it happened. We both stopped, and he said that he wanted to shake my hand.

As we shook, he began telling me some about his experiences in the Army and how he was wounded twice. He went inside and brought out all of his medals that he had received. I couldn't help but see how proud he was to receive a recognition for an accomplishment that he had proudly earned defending his country. It was at that moment when I almost understood his reasons for staying drunk for weeks at a time and his reason for never sharing his past experiences with me until then.

I wouldn't have ever believed or appreciated him or his reason because I had never experienced any of it. He knew, as he had been, that I had been specially trained for the jungle warfare of South Vietnam. After meeting and sharing with Jay, everything else was a blur for me as I walked down each road and remembered what was.

Before meeting the then-unfamiliar military bus in Modesto on January 4, I had sold the 1960 Impala two-door hardtop. Now I had to have a friend with a car stop by for a ride when I needed a tour of this small town to see all the changes that were made while I was gone. The second big thing was a wedding.

As you will recall, when I completed AIT at Fort Polk, I had to call the girl in waiting to let her know that I wasn't coming home very soon. Well, the very soon finally arrived, and I was going to be in my army dress greens. The wedding venue had to be changed to a small church just down the street from her parents' house. The location and time were set, and everything was in place. To my surprise, my parents and a sister did attend and remained, unlike my four graduations. I presumed the venue change, date change, and any other changes I wasn't aware of were part of the reason the wedding was unlike a typical wedding as we know.

It seemed to be fast, and the reception was with a few friends and the family. My in-laws let us use their car to go on a honeymoon. We first went to Yosemite National Park for two or three days. Then to the LA Basin and to Disneyland for two or three days. When we returned to Modesto, it was time for me to pack my belongings again.

Leaving Modesto this time was from the small Modesto Air Terminal where I was joined by my wife of ten days, my parents, and sibling number six, Carol, and her young daughter. While saying our farewells, I did notice that my dad stood in the background from the small family group. I never knew why. My niece Regina noticed her reflection in my brass belt buckle. As kids will, she made a smudge with her finger. Of course, she didn't know how important it was to a soldier to keep the reflection clear.

Getting on board the two-engine prop aircraft for San Francisco was one of the hardest things for me to do. It could have been the last time. As the door closed tight, the turbine engine on the right began turning first. When the hum of it started, the engine on the left began to turn. As the two windmills synchronized their tune, the fuselage began to follow them down the runway, and I waved what very well could have been my last. We began to float in the air toward San Francisco. The humming of the windmills made it difficult to talk to anyone. Besides, I wasn't in the mood to talk anyway.

After a very short flight, we landed at San Francisco International and waited for our next experience. The next journey would be aboard my next flight. After waiting for about an hour, the call came over the intercom for my flight. The flight seemed full as I walked down the very long aisle of this huge plane. When I found my assigned seat, I was sitting between an army captain and a sergeant. We greeted each other and sat back to relax and wait for the flight to Fort Lewis to begin.

It seemed as though this flight sure took a lot more time to get loaded than what was usual. Finally, I heard engine number one pop, and smoke began to exhaust from it as the rpm began to increase. The second engine followed suit. The third then began to exhaust its smoke, but no pop was heard. Soon the fourth one began its hum and was in perfect time with its three partners. The floating as we began to separate from the runway was somewhat rough at first. As the main set of wheels slowly disconnected with the asphalt, we were floating like an eagle with a strong up draft under him.

As the aircraft continued to increase its altitude and we traveled farther and farther from out toward the outer limits, I began to feel really weird. The weirdness was sort of an uncomfortable sick kind. I was an experienced flier. I had flown four times prior to this one and had never felt sick, especially like this. While all these thoughts and reasons were bouncing around in that pea brain I mentioned, I must have begun to change colors as the lizards out in the jungle. The army captain sitting next to the window noticed the change and asked me if I was all right.

Then the army sergeant seated in the aisle seat also noticed. I told them that I felt good, but I don't think they believed me. Almost simultaneously, they both directed the overhead oxygen ports directly on me and told me to relax and breathe. When I recovered, I explained to them the only cause of such an unusual reaction (being a seasoned flyer as I was) that I could think of was a string of sickness called home. I had just left my family and the comfort and security that I had grown up with, and I had gotten married about seven days earlier.

I was entering a phase in my life when I didn't know exactly where I was going or where I would be at any moment. I wasn't sure if I would ever see my family again. As a side note, I then understood how my great-grandparents must have felt being forced to walk the trail of tears and being forced to settle on a strange land called a reservation. When my parents two generations later left the drought-ridden land of Oklahoma to escape the dust bowl days and traveled to an unfamiliar land, leaving family and everything they had and knew behind, they probably felt the same way as I did.

Needless to say, the fresh air that I inhaled did help me feel better. As our craft began to make the final approach and the four wing masters began to adjust their tone and pitch, I could feel a sense of excitement and anticipation and wonder starting to boil up inside of me. The landing was smooth, and we were on the ground back in Seattle. After thanking the captain and sergeant again for their assistance, we each went our separate ways.

Wandering around in the Sea-Tac air terminal, I was approached by a uniformed person who recognized that I must not know where I was or where I was going. Because active members of the armed forces have a special unspoken connection and mutual understanding of each other and the needs of another, it so happened that he was also going to Fort Lewis where he was stationed and said I could ride with him for five dollars. I was thinking (pea brain again) that the five dollars would be helping him pay for his gas in order to get back to the base.

Well, it was in a way. After loading my military-issue suitcase (a duffel bag), we pulled away from the parking lot. He then told me that he provided transportation to Fort Lewis in order to make some extra money for his family. Now that was cool. As his car found its way down the road toward Fort Lewis, there seemed to be a certain familiarity about the road and the surroundings that I just couldn't put my finger on. It was like I had seen this road and the surrounding area before.

As we passed through the main gate at Fort Lewis, the soldier proceeded to take me to an area I did not know. It sure wasn't the North Fort area where I had been for basic training. The drop-off spot was the out-of-country processing center. This center's responsibility was to process paperwork and prepare the soldiers who were being shipped to either South Vietnam or South Korea.

As I entered the building, I saw proctors at every processing station to assist or answer questions. At the first desk near the entrance of the building sat a table with two stacks of forms that were in triplicates. One stack had a sign that was marked Vietnam, and the second stack was for South Korea. Each soldier entering the center had to take the required forms from one of the stacks and fill them out. Keep in mind that during all of my training in Basic, AIT, and APC school, I knew that I was being prepared for a vacation in South Vietnam.

There was actually a clear understanding, but I could not help to wonder what would happen if I took a packet of forms from the South Korea pile. And if I were sent to Korea, I wondered if I would have to stay and do my tour of duty there for the thirteen months. If I did and the person in charge found out that I was supposed to be in Vietnam and not Korea, I wondered if I would have an option to remain Korea or be sent to Vietnam.

It didn't take long for me to get an answer. The second station was where another proctor was seated and asked for my orders. (As a side note, the way the military conducts business a person cannot be transferred or moved to a different unit or area without a transfer order that states who, what, when, and what time of arrival.) The second station proctor received the orders he checked and reviewed the orders. This process kept everyone honest. Needless to say, the Vietnam forms were completed thanks to the checker.

In the late afternoon of that day, the soldiers had completed the process through the processing center and were transported by four buses to McChord Air Force Base. There we were shuffled on board this huge passenger plane. The craft was being filled up with soldiers who had been specially trained and were probably not ready to proceed emotionally but were sure willing to face their objective head on for God, family, and country.

Once again, through the silence that engulfed each seat and soul of every soldier aboard, I began to hear the familiar noise of each engine that hung on the wings and seemed more than ready to be put into an operational mode. As all four began their synchronized humming, silence fell over the inside of the fuselage, and the wind created by the giant engines began to increase. I could feel the ground begin rolling away, allowing the power to move the craft down the runway, which it had done hundreds of times before. As the craft reached near the end of its road, it was lifted up as a balloon full of helium, and we were carried off into a darkened sky and finally disappeared from the sight of the land that we all knew and loved.

Exhausted from the many events and stress of the day, I

tried to catch a nap as the heaviness floated through the seats, teasing each of us. I must have lost track of the time while fighting with the nap as it tried to engulf me. Our plane began its long approach to its next nest and resting place. Just prior to touching down, a voice came over the intercom and said that we were making a refueling stop at Tokyo, and we would not be allowed to disembark and get lost.

As the plane descended and we got closer to the ground, I looked out the small window and could see the headlight of a few cars reflecting on to the road and seemingly glowing into the darkness. It's funny; I had never seen or even thought of the lights of a car shining and moving along the road as the driver directed the position and direction of their glowing movements.

The fuel trucks must have been waiting for our arrival. The refueling process only took about thirty to forty-five minutes. While the refueling was going on, the silence inside the plane was interrupted by someone offering us something to drink. Our choices would be to help nourish our bodies and nothing to lift up our mellow spirits.

After about forty-five minutes, we were once again listening to the whining of the four jet engines as each of them inhaled the Tokyo night air. Soon we were off and up into the darkness that we knew not. I must have lost track of time again. It didn't seem much longer before the plane was making another approach. This landing would be on the soil of a country that I had never heard of, didn't know anyone in, and really didn't care too much about. On June 26, 1968, the aircraft made a safe and soft landing at Cam Rhan Bay, South Vietnam, which ended the journey, taking each of us away from our homes and dropping us off in a small country in Southeast Asia that almost no one knew anything about.

After unloading and stepping onto this strange land, we were taken to yet another receiving station that processed us into this country. After the required paperwork and forms were filled out and completed, we were taken to the living quarters to await further orders. After my first military meal in this country, I met two soldiers who were from the state of Virginia. Just like California, Virginia was a world away now.

Ira Caldwell was the first guy I met, and we became friends and hung out together. The second day or so, Ira and I met and became friends with Ronald Conklin. Ron was known as Virginia, so the name continued a half-world away. The Cam Rhan receiving station was a temporary stop.

While at the receiving station, Ira and I made an attempt to volunteer to be door gunners on the helicopter operation during our tour. We were told that we had to have six months in country before we would be considered. After we had been in combat for six months and saw what was happening, we changed our minds. On the third or fourth day, the three amigos received our orders and finally knew that we were assigned to the First Cavalry Division, Seventh Cavalry Regiment, and B Company.

As a side note, if you remember some of American history, you can recall General

George Custer's Battle of the Little Bighorn against Chief Sitting Bull and the Sioux Indians, as well as the other various Native American tribes. Well, General Custer's unit was the Seventh Cavalry. When the three amigos found out that we were being placed in the Seventh Cavalry, I told my buddies that I wasn't going to fight Custer's Last Stand.

During the following two weeks, we were in a mini basic training. During this short training session, we repelled from towers, exercised, and became oriented to the culture of this country. We were also instructed on what not to do while "guests" of these people and helping them. Things we were taught here were to treat them with respect, do not abuse them, treat their water buffalo as sacred, and anything after that I must not have listened. During this lesson, I whispered to Ira, "If we are guests here, why are we being mistreated and killed?" We did receive a lot of instructions on the culture, crops, and land of these simple, hard-working people. I believe that this mini training was not only to orient us to the people and country but also to allow each of us to become acclimated to the higher humidity and heat of the country and region.

After the two weeks of training, the three amigos and a dozen or so other soldiers were loaded onto a C-123 twin-engine transporter aircraft and flown to the northern region. As the twin-engine craft made its approach to Camp Evans, I looked out and saw the lush, thick green of the trees and bushes that were around the LZ (landing zone) area. Camp Evans is near the Northern Village of Quan Loi, which is close to the base of the mountain region just South of the DMZ (Demilitarized Zone) separating South Viet Nam from the Communist North. After about four days at Camp Evans, it was time for deployment.

We all packed up our gear and belongings and were at the ready. It wasn't very long before we saw six Huey helicopters about to land on the airstrip. The airstrip had two wreckages of C-130 four-engine transporters at the end of the runway. As the choppers made their approach to land, the dirt was swirled around, creating a dust storm and an illusion that the C-130s had just, at that moment, crashed. I managed to take a few pictures of the scene. Unlike the Seventh Cavalry in General Custer's days when horses were used for transportation, the modern-day Cavalry used the Huey helicopter and air. We were going to be air mobile.

Being air mobile, we could respond and be moved more quickly. We climbed into the opened doors of the chopper, and we were off into the Vietnam skies. We had no idea where we were going. After a thirty-minute flight, the choppers began to land. We all jumped out, and they were off to pick up a second group to be joined with us.

While the choppers were gone, we had to provide security for the troops and choppers when they returned with the second load. When the last group arrived, we formed up in our platoon groups and began walking and patrolling. Still only the leaders knew where we were going. Probably about two miles after we began our stroll, we approached and could see the Pacific Ocean.

Now that was a little weird. As we got closer to the water, we could see a series of bunkers arranged in a horseshoe shape on the beach area. Because I was placed in a different squad than Ron and Ira, I didn't see them, but I did hear someone say or make a statement like, "What in the hell are we doing here?" I really didn't care. I love the ocean and the beauty of the surroundings. We later found out that this was Wonder Beach and a small naval post to receive supplies.

Two soldiers were assigned to each bunker to provide security for this area. After a couple of days, one of our guys found out that the navy personnel were eating hot meals and watching movies every night, while we provided security and got to eat our C- rations. Each part of the meal was contained in a can, which made transporting it easy and helped the contents last.

So because this didn't seem fair, we asked the field captain to ask if we could watch a movie with them. We would have to do so on a rotating basis because of the security responsibility. He did ask, they said yes. One soldier from three or four bunkers each night would join the navy for a "date night." After a week or so, we returned to the drop-off area from a week earlier to meet the choppers again. We again did not know exactly what the destination was, but we knew the ocean vacation was over.

Arriving at our destination, the choppers hovered over the grassy clearing as we jumped out. I jumped out, being the last out behind the men of the squad. I had a weird feeling that because the ocean vacation had ended, it was now to begin the job that I knew I was trained for. One by one, the men of the squad disappeared as each wandered into the thickness of the bushes and the overgrown grass. After walking in the heat with our sixty-pound backpacks for a long distance, we stopped for a break. One of the squad members, Ronald Bolden, saw that I was drinking my water too fast. He offered me a drink from his canteen and told me how to drink and conserve water while managing to deal with the heat and humidity. He explained to take one big mouth full, swish it around inside, and then swallow very slowly and enjoy it as long as I could. That advice was probably one of the most important and helpful things that I received and learned from.

As the first day came to an end for our group outing, we found a suitable place to set up a camp and our security perimeter. We set out the trip flairs and security wiring. The next morning the company broke camp and began to move to our next destination. As the lead squad began moving and clearing the trail, the point man and his backup began to receive weapons fire.

We set up a guarded perimeter until the situation was cleared. We were stopped for a couple of hours or more. When everything had been cleared, the report was that two lead soldiers had been killed along with the Vietcong sniper. The third person was severely wounded. The medevac chopper arrived a short time later to extract the bodies and the wounded. While we were waiting, I made a grave mistake. The cardinal rule about combat is to not write home about anything related to a combat situation. I wrote to my parents; however, they never mentioned receiving the letter or knowing about the situation. While we were stopped and waiting for the extracting chopper, I did write home about the situation and added that I was going try to transfer to a chaplain unit.

The transfer did not happen. A second letter about what was actually going on did not either. As I reflect back on a dismal period in all American lives, especially mine, I do recall that a few months after the squad experienced two sniper attacks, the company's concentrated efforts were focused on the mountain region south of the DMZ.

When doing our patrols to flush out the enemy and secure the area, our platoon would rotate and trade places with other platoons in our company. The rotation meant we would have our turn securing the top of the highest area of the range, known as LZ Helen. While we were at the LZ (landing zone) atop the highest section, we would be able to receive our mail and any goodie boxes to share, along with some rest. This rest stop would last about three days.

Chapter 7

One wild visit that we had on the mountaintop was during the Vietnam wintertime. My squad was in a sandbag bunker that sat on the edge of the mountain cliff. The bunker was not completely finished on the backside. We were supposed to complete the exposed side during our visit. We spent one whole day just filling issued bags with dirt. As the bags were filled, a couple of the guys were stacking and building the missing wall. None of the squad men had asked these two about having any building construction experience. As the bags were filled, the wall was erected. As the new bagged wall met the overhanging roof, we felt very proud. Now we were experienced builders and bag fillers. As the night became colder, the winds began to rise up and became colder as mountain air and wind do. As the darkness really fell hard, so did the bags filled with mountain dirt.

I don't know if the wind was too strong or the construction was not strong enough. We were awakened by the cold wind tickling our noses and ears as it sneaked through the holes and spaces now existing in our newly constructed project. When a person gets cold, what is the best thing to do? Do whatever it takes to get warm, right? Well, the same was true for us. But how? One of the squad members recalled that the mess hall tent had just received a few five-gallon cans of fuel used to clean eating utensils and plates. With the mess tent being closed, he volunteered to "fuel-nap" one of the cans. Although we did not know what kind of fuel was used for cleaning, we all invited the can in our bunker to become our warming friend.

The liquid inside the can did have a familiar odor, but who really cared. We were too cold to care. Each squad man filled his iron helmet pot with the fuel and lit it, and then we waited for the heat to float throughout our dark, cold prison and share its warmth. The fuel did seem to be willing to share its warmth and comfort with us as we sat close to the small flame. Almost in unison, each of us moved closer to the helmet pot with hopes to intercept the heat as it escaped and rose up into the coolness of our night air.

As the darkness moved and made room for the dawn to begin another humid day, each one of us exited our night in prison to breathe some fresh air and start another day. As each of us emerged from the cold bunker, we were greeted with pointing and laughter. We all wondered what they were laughing at. Our newly constructed wall had fallen during the night, we thought we would be frozen, and now they were laughing. When the platoon sergeant saw us, he almost laughed and told us to get cleaned up. *Oh good*, I thought, *breakfast is ready*. As we each began to wash, we were able to see our reflections in a small mirror that hung near the water supply. We had to laugh at each other as we washed.

If you have ever driven behind a school bus or diesel truck, you know that black plumes of smoke are exhausted and can cover everything. Well, we were no exception to the rule. To our amazement, each of us was coated with black soot on our hands, arms, hair, and especially our faces. The magic fuel that had been retrieved to deliver its warmth and comfort to us as we suffered through the night was diesel fuel. Need I say more?

Another fun time my squad had was during another turn that we had on top of the mountain. With our bunker location on the other side of the ridge, we went to visit another bunker area to socialize. I am not sure why, but we all transformed in our minds to become entertainers. Like all performers, we had to choose and mutually agreed on a song. The chosen song was "Donna" by Richie Valens. Somehow, we began the song together at the same time. Just imagine First Cavalry soldiers on top of the mountain in the Ashau Valley trying to sing "Donna." The VC must have been laughing their helmets off at our attempt. There were probably a few who were even howling like a dog when its ears hurt from the noise.

On one occasion while we were off the mountain but ready to return, our company was sent to an area we called The Bridges. They were two foot bridges that spanned across a small river. One of them was wide enough for a small vehicle to drive across with items such as rifles, mortars, or other items of mass destruction to a small area. While performing our guard duties, our encampment area was a small distance from the danger zone.

Every day while we were there, youngsters from the nearby village would stop by our fenced area. The preteens would engulf the outside of the protective gate to talk and at least try to learn the language and sell their wares. The major portion of the products they tried to sell was a liquor simulation of VO whiskey. Other items were knives, picture frames, pouches, and anything else they could get their hands on. One of the guys traded a case of C-rations for two bottles of their watered-down VO. Two of the boys wanted someone to adopt them and take them to America.

Another event occurred while we were in the valley camped at an LZ. One of the soldiers "borrowed" two cases of rations and traded them to a local villager for a freezer storage bag almost full of marijuana. Remember, we were treading around this country in 1968. One day before we returned to our mountain range mission, just before the dawning slapped us, the LZ began receiving incoming mortar rounds. The group that was smoking didn't seem to care what was happening. My Navajo Indian buddy Richard and I were near those who were floating high. As the mortars began to hit and explode, Richard and I forcefully shoved the party boys to the entry of the bunker and made sure they were inside.

Later we were transported by choppers back to the mountains. While patrolling an area we had been through a month or so earlier, our point man noticed something like a barrier that looked very unusual. As we removed the unusual barrier, we could see a carved-out cave. As we inspected, the cave we found was a field hospital that had been dug out on the side of a mountain. We recovered a massive amount of wrappings and medications for pain, along with a large amount of needles and other hospital supplies. We determined that this makeshift hospital was used to treat and patch up a wounded VC soldier before sending him to the rear. The beds of the hospital were also carved from the dirt walls of the mountains.

As we departed the hospital, we had to throw a few fragmentation grenades into the facility to destroy it.

As I recall, in about February 1969, our squad count was down from ten or twelve to five. Our company commander told the five of us to set up an outpost near a well-traveled foot trail that we happened to come upon. When the company stopped for that night, the five of us proceed to our designated location very close to this well-used trail. We did what we did every night when a camp was set up. We dug three very deep foxholes and aligned our trip flairs around our perimeter overlapping each other.

The mortar platoon sergeant was contacted by the GI phone because carrier pigeons would have had difficulty maneuvering through the thick, overgrown terrain. He assured us that if needed, he could drop a round within three feet of our location. As the five of us sat and waited, the black of the night began to engulf us. Richard and I were occupying one of the foxhole locations. We were determined to make sure the other three stayed awake. As the night fell upon us, we became more alert and the situation became more intense.

Our commander received word that a battalion of VC troops were expected to be coming down the large path. We didn't know if they were coming or not, but we were ready. As the night grew darker and we grew wearier, we began to doubt the purpose. About midnight or one o'clock, one of the trip flare wires was hit, and the whole surrounding area lit up as if the sun was smiling down on us. We knew that our invitation had been discovered and accepted, and we were ready to greet our guest. As our frag grenades found their way to the noise on the small road, we could hear a language that we did not understand. As another grenade found the trail, more noise was heard. Some of the voices seemed to be very close. The mortar tubs dropped one mortar on their location but chose not to after that one because the flash of the mortar tube could be seen as it broke through the darkness. This intense fighting in the dark seemed to carry on into the coming dawn.

However, it actually lasted about two hours. As the morning light began to filter through the thickness of the overgrown vines and bushy trees, another squad of men joined the five of us to check out any damages. In this very fertile grassy land, the six-foot tall strands of grass were lying against the ground for as far as we could see. On most of the lazy grass, we saw blood about every two feet. We also found an AK-47 assault weapon, a few Russian-made grenades, and a few helmets. We knew that the night traveling group gathered their wounded, because we did not find any bodies. Of the grenades that were thrown that night, I only had one left on my pack strap. The others were completely out. We were sure glad to pack our things and move on to the next adventure.

A person who serves his country in a combat zone becomes very battle fatigued while facing and experiencing and living in conflict 24/7. A time-out of sorts is usually scheduled after six months in the field. The R&R (rest and relaxation) is both earned and looked forward to by a combat soldier. I was no different. My R&R, however, was scheduled nine months after I entered this country due to the amount of contact we had experienced. I wrote about getting married a week before I left my family and comfort to go to the unknown. It so happened that my first wife had a high school friend who married a sailor, and they were stationed in Hawaii in 1969. I had never been to paradise and thought with my wife's friend being stationed there Hawaii would be an ideal place to meet.

My wife arrived a few days before me and spent time with her friend. When I arrived, I was met at the airport and taken to the hotel. I had been looking forward to seeing her and being with her for nine long months. She was a very welcomed sight. I had almost forgotten what she looked like. She was definitely a bright light to the darkness I had been in. A schedule of special events and things to do was made, so we laid out our plans to tour and view. After the first day of not being seen by anyone, we rented a 1969 Chevy Chevelle and began touring. As it so happened the movie *Tora! Tora! Tora!* (Japanese terms for attack, attack, attack) was being filmed. The excellent movie depicted the air attack on Pearl Harbor. While we were driving, I saw the single-engine attack bombers belonging to the country of Japan. Just coming from a combat zone, I thought the islands were being attacked again. As I was preparing to respond, I heard on the car's radio about the filming and not to worry.

What a shock to see these planes up close. A day or two later, we toured the USS *Arizona* Memorial. What an interesting venue. The USS *Arizona* was the American battleship that was torpedoed by the attack planes during a surprise attack and then sunk in the Pearl Harbor where it was had been. The memorial is a must-see when you visiting the area.

We also visited Hawaii's beautiful sites and enjoyed being together. As time continued to pass, the week that I spent in paradise came to an end too soon. Having to say farewell to my new bride was a very difficult thing. She was sending a very renewed soldier back to complete his mission.

As I boarded my return flight, I took my assigned seat, but I couldn't help thinking about how I was leaving paradise to return to a hell that I did not understand. Was there something wrong with my thinking? I did have the thought of not returning to do what I despised. But, I remembered that my forefathers did not give up or turn back from their purpose.

Chapter 8

Probably about four weeks after returning to the hell and my squad, everything seemed to be very different. There were new recruits in our platoon, and the company was patrolling a new and unfamiliar territory. On the April 17, 1969, as our platoon moved slowly through the thickest and most overgrown area of the jungle, the second platoon came upon an occupied bunker complex. As their platoon leader directed each squad to a position of safety, he was shot three times and fell into the bomb crater that he was standing on the edge of.

My First Platoon leader came over to my secured perimeter position and asked me to go to the crater and pull the lieutenant out. He had to be kidding, right? Of course he wasn't. Though I was getting to be a short-timer (a person who has thirty days or less in country), I figured if it was my time, it would happen here. While under fire, I crawled into the deep, rocky crater and saw that Lieutenant Racca, Second Platoon Leader, was severely wounded. As I carried him out of the crater, I reassured him that he would be okay and would be going home. However, as I carried him up the grade of the hill to the medevac pad, his gurgling stopped. I knew then for sure that he was going home.

The circumstances of that situation have haunted me for forty-three years—just not knowing much about him or his family. However, in 2012, that all ended. I was able to locate and contact his family members. It seemed that a heavy weight had been removed from my shoulders. Back in the combat field, I recall about a month or so after retrieving the severely wounded Lieutenant Racca from the bomb crater, the platoon sergeant sent for me. I knew it was not yet time for me to mount the bird to be flown back to the world, so I could imagine why I would be called upon. The sergeant knew that I had been out in the field for ten months or more and had also participated in all the firefights that the company was involved in up to that time. He was aware of the fact that I was with the company each time that we had made the almost two hundred combat assaults, and most of them had been into a hot LZ.

Though there was never a complaint, the battle fatigue must have been showing, because as I approached his location, he handed me a slip of paper, similar to a large concert or movie ticket. I asked him what the paper was for, because I always carried more than my share of responsibility. I wondered why he would give this paper to me if it was to go to someone else. I asked him what it was for, and he said that I had been given a three-day in-country R&R.

I had been aware of the First Cavalry's in-country R&R program but never thought that I would be blessed to receive one. After the sergeant explained the minor details of the short R&R for some rest and relaxation, I anxiously waited for the arrival of the morning chopper to whisk me away, even if it was going to be only for a few days. I had no idea where this R&R Center was or what to expect when I arrived.

The chopper finally arrived, and it was like a golden eagle that was only going to take me, a combat infantry man of very little importance, to an area to relax and get away from the everyday grind of battle and digging foxholes. Needless to say, it did not take me but a heartbeat to jump on the hard, cold metal floor of this delivery bird. The chopper landed at the air force–occupied LZ, close to the small runway landing strip where sat the somewhat larger chopper used for LZ-to-LZ landing.

I was joined on the tarmac area by a few other soldiers who were from other First Cavalry units. It's funny how things work out even in a combat zone. As a few of us came together into a small group, we greeted each other because we were "brothers for the cause" and had no reason not to greet each other.

A soldier from the Ninth Cavalry named Jim and I began talking and sharing. I'm sure that he was just as insecure and anxious as I was about the short R&R trip. As Jim of the Ninth Cavalry and I both landed on the short-term freedom flight, we were still anticipating what lay ahead for us in the unknown. We had faced the unknown before when we stepped on the soil of this small country that was not known to many people or even heard of by all. So we figured that having to face our anxiety with a short vacation would surely be much easier and more fun than what we had faced for the previous ten months.

The First Cavalry R&R center in Vietnam was small coastal town of Vong Tau. This R&R center was quite a welcomed change of environment from what we had been accustomed to. As I got an overview of the area with Jim, I saw that the area seemed to be a fun and enjoyable area with a lot of entertainment and things to do. And with the town and center being on the ocean's shores, it reminded me somewhat of a toned-down version of Santa Cruz, California, a central coast beach town that has a magnetic draw of people, especially the youth.

One of the many things this unique area had that was in the view of passersby and known by the people who lived in the surrounding areas was the legality and openness of the century-old profession of prostitution. Jim and I decided to do some hiking and see what we could discover that would not be a booby trap or land mine, as when my unit the Seventh Cavalry had the security detail at The Bridges and the village male kids came to our compound and tried to sell their goods to make money either for themselves or their families. There were two young boys in Vung Tau who wanted to be assistance to us. For a price, of course.

The only thing that they could assist us with and that we wanted to trust them with was to carry our boots for us when needed. So they followed along with us. As tour guides do, the assistants suggested and led us up a small hill area where we saw a large statue of a Buddha watching over the village. As Jim and I approached the symbolic statue, the loyal guides began to be persistent about us removing our footwear. I asked them why we should take our boots off to walk on the marble-looking surface surrounding the statue. One of the youngsters told us that the ground was holy and should not be walked on.

I told the boys that we were not Buddhist and the ground was not holy to us. After some additional persuasion from the boys, Jim and I decided not to disrespect their belief and feeling for the symbol. I recall that we were briefed on this subject when we first entered the country. So we removed our boots, and the boys carried them for us as we walked around among the well-groomed trees and shrubs that provided shade for those who took the time to visit the shrine. We were under the shade as we walked around the small hill and continued our hiking expedition to discover what we dared to.

As we were lacing up our boots, our young friends asked us if we wanted "boom." Neither of us knew what they were talking about, but as we entered the city area while we backtracked to where we had started from, one of the assistants pointed to a building with Vietnamese writing on a sign and told us "boom." Jim said maybe it was a restaurant or a bar. When asked, and one of the boys told us what the words meant. So putting two and two together, we quickly realized that the structure was not a restaurant but a brothel. Jim and I declined their offer. We decided to return to the cavalry complex and get some food that we were familiar with before looking around more.

While in the complex area, I saw a tailor shop. Knowing that I was going to college and on into criminology and realizing that formal dinners and award ceremonies would require formal attire, I inquired about the clothing. The suits and other clothing items were all made in Hong Kong and had a two- or three-day delivery time. Without considering my size at the time and any future weight development, I went in for a fitting measurement. I ended up ordering one suit made of silk, if I recall correctly, and two tuxedo jackets, one light sky blue with a black lace covering the light-blue material and one white and also having the black lace over the white. I also purchased two oriental-style smoking jackets.

Should we ever meet, please don't ask me why I purchased such unusual tux jackets. I had known from birth I was a little different after weighing in at twelve pounds. As I grew older, the confirmation was clear. I would probably never use the black-lace-covered tuxedo jacket. Although they were made well and looked good, they both would be very different from any other tuxedo jacket ever made. In addition, I never calculated any possible changes in my weight while attending college or working my career after returning to my homeland. All of this means that I never wore either tuxedo jacket, but they sure added a brilliant color dimension to the clothes that hung in my closet.

Jim and I spent some time on the shore of the Pacific Ocean as we waded out into the cooling wet waters that even touched the California shores. The beach areas were very sandy, and I noticed that not as many people were out enjoying the surf as there are on the beaches of United States. The reason for this could possibly be that due to the war, only a small number of the wealthier could take the time to enjoy such a luxury. Our time at the cavalry complex was very relaxing for Jim and me both. We did have a good time, considering where we were. Upon returning to the designated base camp, we met two other troopers who were also returning from the cavalry complex but had been at the base one day before Jim and I arrived.

The four of us stuck together and slept in the air force barracks area prior to deciding to return to our company's area. While there, it seems that our companies had come under heavy mortar and rocket attacks. Each morning there was only room for one or two persons after the needed supplies were loaded onto the twin-engine Caribou transporter. In order to get a space on the Caribou, a person had to be at the loading area at five thirty in the morning. Of course, none of the four of us were very anxious to get back to our units with all the fire action going on. So after we would have a good air force breakfast, we would take our time going down to the required area.

We would arrive about seven o'clock each morning. After being asked why we were late by the transport sergeant, we were given AF details. These details consisted of cleaning the barracks area, dumping trash, and any other duty that the airman could find for us. After two or three days of being late for transporting out of our resting area, we decided that the time had come for us to return and join our groups and get things on the ground back in order. So off we went on the fourth day.

Many other events occurred during the year that I spent on this wild adventure. Most of them have been locked in my memory by time. The others, I choose not to recall.

One muggy day the chopper brought supplies to our company out in the field. This day was a day I had been anxiously waiting for. As the craft landed and the supplies were unloaded, the platoon sergeant called my name. Being unaware of the date, I reported to him. He asked me, "Do you want to see the world?" In other words, he was asking if I was ready to go home. I picked up my pack and ran to the chopper as it waited for me. The chopper flew me to our base camp. From there, I boarded a twin-engine light transporter craft called a Caribou. The engine began to roar, and before very long, we were in the air on our way to An Khê. The town of An Khê was the First Cavalry Division Headquarters. This military base is the location that every soldier looks forward to be at.

There was a processing station there similar to the one at Fort Lewis. The An Khê Station processes each soldier who served in the First Cavalry Division out of the battle-torn country of South Vietnam. After doing the paperwork for leaving this country, three other guys (Ronald, Ira, and Jim) and I were placed in a transit barracks. In this single-story building, we had to wait for our orders to depart from this hell. For a total of three days, the four of us were kept at this area waiting. Each of those days, the four of us were inspected and sent to the barber on base to get our hair trimmed.

The second time we had it cut, the barber left nothing else to be cut. If we would have had to go see the barber a fourth time, our heads would have been shaved down to the skin. After spending the worst year of our lives in a war-torn country that we could barely find on the map, we sure didn't want to stay any longer that we had to. Finally, the day had come. Our orders were in hand, and we four were called to get on board a long-range Tiger Airline's four-engine jet that would take us to freedom and back to the land that we called "the world."

When the airliner was completely filled with men who had been fighting a political conflict for twelve months, I heard engine number one repeat the almost-forgotten sound as in the beginning—the turning over to start. Engine number two repeated number one, as did three and four. Soon, all four engines were humming and anxiously waited for the runway okay.

Once at the beginning of the runway, we did not start moving toward the end as most flights do. When I looked out the window, there seemed to be a dark blanket of rain washing over the aircraft. During the twenty of thirty minutes we sat there on the plane waiting for the monsoon storm to pass over us, I couldn't help to think that the plane would make a good target for the enemy if they chose to use us as one. After probably the longest twenty or so minutes I had ever experienced of sitting there and waiting, the engines began to hum a different tune as the plane began to taxi down the wet runway. I finally heard the welcoming sound of the rubber tires seeming to struggle as they separated from the asphalt. The craft began the freedom lift.

As we floated higher and higher, I knew we were homeward bound. Wouldn't you know, even though the storm passed over us while waiting patiently on the ground, it must have been waiting for our departure. As the craft lifted higher and higher, we had to penetrate through the heavy, thick, black wetness of the clouds before we could proceed on our way. As we passed through the lightless night of the storm, the wings of the plane appeared to be flapping as a bird in flight as it conquered its way through the turbulence of the storm.

The sight of the plane trying to be in flight as a bird really freaked me out. After being in this small, unknown country for just over a year and surviving, I sure didn't want everything to come to an end in this confusing darkness of the storm. However, if my life was to end there, I wouldn't have as far to travel to be home.

Finally, the light of the day broke through, and I knew that we had been delivered from a storm that seemingly didn't want us to leave. As I recall, the pilot landed the plane in Guam, a 209-square-mile area that is an unincorporated territory of the United States, to refuel and take on other supplies, including food and drink items. I doubt if food supplies would have been necessary on this trip, because all of the troopers on this flight were too tired, too thankful, and too excited to think about nourishment.

Hours and hours after the four engines of this long-range jet echoed their concert songs through the night skies, we finally began our approach. We weren't sure where the approach was to be or where we were going to land. None of the soldiers were concerned about where we would be landing, as long as it was on US soil. As the plane slowed and the ground became closer and closer to us, the pilot announced that we would be landing in Oakland, California. Anticipation and anxiety levels were so high that I thought any one of us may explode. It's a feeling that cannot be written down on paper for someone to read or understand what the landing really meant. Unless there is personal experience of something of this magnitude and importance, a person never would know the true inner feeling of a person in our boots.

As we all stepped off this long and tiring flight, we were filled with joy and excitement to such a high level that most of the guys actually kissed the ground. They were so happy and thrilled to be finally back on American soil. After disembarking the flight, we were escorted to an area near the terminal, similar to the areas we had seen before, to be processed back into our own country

The Oakland receiving station was much larger than the previous ones. I guess the size of this station was because of the number of soldiers returning from overseas deployments and being a military base. One of the joys of returning, besides being on American soil and having it meet us as the plane touched down, was the breakfast at three o'clock in the morning consisting of eggs and a thick, juicy steak and our chose of beverage.

The four musketeers who'd left the small battle-torn country about twelve hours earlier now sat at the breakfast table together and savored the very delicious meal that we had missed out on for the entire year. Unlike in basic training, we had all the time that we needed to eat. After all the savoring was complete, we were taken into the processing area to process the paperwork for reentry into our beloved country.

When the reentry process was completed, we were taken to the all-familiar green bus, which transported us to San Francisco International Airport. The other soldiers who were on the return flight also processed back into the country, but due to the anxiety and excitement of being back at home, I don't know what direction they were drawn to. I just hope they all made it home.

The four of us made the trip across the bay and south on Highway 101 to the airport. Arriving at the terminals, I accompanied the other three guys to their airport destinations one at a time. As we walked from one terminal to another, we did not receive a welcome home from those who passed by us. We were punctured by visual daggers and snarls. One person even spit in our direction. I wanted to go over to him to "have a talk," but I was so happy to be back on familiar soil that I had second thoughts. I was stopped by Ira pulling on my arm to stop my advance. We continued counting our stepping forward. We were also called baby killers, because of the news coverage of what they wanted the home front to see.

Today, we Vietnam veterans clearly remember how we were treated and the ugly names we were called as we returned from our tours of duty. Upon my return, I personally experienced some of the harsh feelings that that many of my ancestors must have experienced generations before. As our troops today return from their tours in the Middle East and Africa, the Vietnam veteran will almost always be present to greet them home, serve them, and plan an event to include them.

Chapter 9

U pon arriving at San Francisco, I had called my wife to come meet me prior to accompanying my buddies to their gates. After seeing the three companions off to their flights, I had to wait about an hour for my wife and her girlfriend to arrive after driving the hour and a half from Modesto. Not many words were spoken during our trip home. I knew that I had enjoyed our time together in Hawaii and that my feelings of love for her were in place. Just how much and how strong, I wasn't sure.

As with all persons who go off to war, various experiences and what has been seen must be dealt with. At this point, my concern was to start our lives and become readjusted back into some sort of lifestyle. Needless to say, I was very happy to see her again and to build any future that would await us. We arrived at the apartment that she had chosen and moved into before visiting parents and other relatives the next day. After getting reacquainted, I soon realized that nothing was the same as I'd left it. She seemed to be the same person whom I'd left, but I had returned home a very changed person.

I knew that I had to readjust into the lifestyle and ways of civilian life when I completed my active duty in the army. In the meantime, I had to follow the written orders I was given prior to getting on board the Tiger Lines jet in An Khê. As my basic training assignment in Washington State was a long way from Modesto, my next duty assignment was Fort Dix, New Jersey, which was three thousand miles from California. How would we get there? We had to go car shopping.

We remembered the 1969 Chevy Chevelle that we rented while in Hawaii and how cool it was. We drove by a used car lot that had a 1967 Chevelle with a black exterior and red interior with bucket seats. I knew I had to have it. The deal was made, and a few days later, the '67 was packed and ready for the next leg of our journey. After saying good-bye to everyone, the car was on the Freeway 99 heading north toward Interstate 80. Interstate 80 is the middle northern route that runs from San Francisco across to United States to New Jersey. The Interstate 80 corridor has beautiful scenery the entire length.

We arrived at Fort Dix about four days later, and I visited the office that assists returning soldiers locate off-post housing. We found a small apartment in the nearby town of Browns Mills. My assigned duty while serving Fort Dix was as a platoon leader. The leader was to assist the drill instructor in the training of basic trainees. From the first day with my platoon, our drill instructor was on leave due to marital problems. That meant it was my responsibility to wake the men up every morning, get them fed, and see to it that they received the required training and their shots and after-training events. As the training cycle continued, so did the testing that comes along with all schooling.

I was assigned to C Company, which only had two platoons, just as the Fort Lewis Basic Training Company that I was in did. The second platoon leader, Greg, had just returned from his vacation in Southeast Asia. The two platoons worked together and helped each other during the obstacle courses, weapons training, and classroom studies. That is the same system that Greg and I were taught during our training. During the physical agility testing of the trainees, after seven weeks of training, Greg and I were pleasantly surprised. After the testing the results were posted, C Company's results were much higher than the other three companies in our battalion. On the weekend of open house, the men seemed to be very anxious to introduce Greg and me to their families. I was very flattered. But on two occasions while I assigned to Fort Dix, I was placed on funeral duty. Being a combat veteran who had just returned after a twelve-month tour myself, I was actually shocked and filled with sorrow for the way that the two men chose to end their lives. To make things worse, nothing could be said to the families to comfort them during their loss.

On both occasions, a trainee from a neighboring battalion committed suicide and was given a military burial with honors. The duty was an honor and a great education for me. I was somewhat taken aback when I heard about the deaths of the two men. They were starting their lives and had a lot to live for. However, I was able to learn and participate in the Honor Guard ceremonies for the two fallen soldiers. I consider it a true honor to have that responsibility bestowed on me. Although the two funerals marked solemn and tragic events, there were some fun times also.

Probably one of the funniest stories that I can relate is about the well-known GI party. In order to set the stage for the story, it's important to understand that at the end of each training cycle, the barracks that housed the personnel being trained had to be cleaned, sanitized, and spit-shined.

This process occurs at every military training facility in the military system. One week, as a neighboring company completed its training cycle, a fellow cadre member and I were told to join other staffers and assist with the GI party.

We complied and were busy with the cleaning, sanitizing, and buffing until about eleven o'clock that night. While the other staffers and I were busy cleaning, my wife arrived at my company to give me a ride home. After being told that we had extra duty, she returned to our home. Greg and I returned after the cleaning was completed to our company to check out for the day.

Because the time was close to midnight, I decided to walk home instead of having my wife make a return trip to retrieve me. Upon arriving home, I explained the cleaning process that we had to work through and the difficulties we had all encountered. It is funny now, but at the time it wasn't. She became very upset when she was told that I was at a GI party. Her interpretation of a party was very different than the military's. The walk home was about five or six miles. Because I had returned from my tour in South Vietnam only a few months before, the distance was not difficult.

About ten weeks prior to being discharged from active duty, I was summoned to the battalion commander's office. When I arrived, I had to wait for the previous appointment to be completed. About ten minutes passed when I saw my company training partner, Second Platoon Sergeant Greg as he came out of the colonel's office. Without saying anything, I could tell from the look on his face that something was up. After knocking on the commanding officer's office door, I entered and was at the position of attention reporting to him.

I knew that the colonel had also just returned from his tour of duty in Vietnam. After being asked to be seated, the chat that I thought we were going to have went like this. He began by congratulating me on the scores and success of my platoon's performance during the training cycle. He asked about my future plans after I told him that I wasn't going to reenlist, which was actually his objective. I told him about my future plans to further my education and be the first of eight kids in the family to complete college. Because I had a two-year degree, I did want to further pursue an education. After briefly discussing education, he asked me about the possibilities of reenlisting and receiving a five thousand-dollar signing bonus. After discussing reenlisting and the bonus, he probably saw that I was definite with my college plans.

He stated that he could order me to go to drill instructor (DI) school with the explanation that the army needed truly committed people who really cared about the trainees and army personnel. He added that records would show that all trainees' performances on tests and cooperation was reflective back on the platoon sergeant. My platoon and Greg's platoon had the highest results in the battalion. I was thinking to myself that every training sergeant probably heard the same song.

I was flattered that a lieutenant colonel would take interest in my abilities to offer such. I again had to decline his offer. My response to his statement was that he could order me to the drill instructor training, and I would do my best but the training was another eight weeks of basic. Because I only had ten weeks left in service and a person being discharged was given one week to clear post, which I was going to take in order to finalize each section such as medical clearance, finances, supplies, being fitted for new dress uniform, and tying up any loose ends.

Because I was taking the full week to clear all the sections, I would only have one week remaining to serve as a DI. To me, that one week would be a waste of my time and the army's time. Out of fairness, I did relate to him that my wife was antimilitary and desperately wanted to be around her family in California.

After another encouraging attempt, he must have seen that

I was firm on my decision. As I was about to leave his office, he shook my hand and wished me well. During the week I was using to clear up each section, I had time to make a call to an Army Medical Center in Michigan to inquire about a Vietnam buddy Harold Cline, whom I'd served with and had been severely wounded and flown home. Hence, I lost touch with him.

I knew he'd been from a town in Pennsylvania, probably Saltsburg. But due to privacy issues, they could only tell me that he had been discharged. Returning to California in early January 1970, I had to take the old Highway 66, which is now I-40, across the country on the southern route to enjoy the sights.

Chapter 10

After arriving back to the winter warmth of Modesto, I had, in a sense, completed a cycle of my life. That is, being drafted and leaving my familiar town and surroundings. Two years later, after experiencing the many things that I had, I was returning to a seemingly unfamiliar town. The cycle was completed, I thought. Without knowing that I needed to adjust back to civilian life a week after beginning to settle into an apartment, I contacted the owner of the Phillips 66 service station I had worked for two years earlier. I also returned to Campbell Soup Company to see if the company had any openings.

I found out from Campbell's human resources department that when a person was drafted who previously had worked for them and wanted to return to a position, the federal statues required that a job had to be offered to the person. The position that HR had for this returning soldier was on a cleanup crew.

The Modesto division of Campbell Soup produced and assembled Swanson brand TV dinners, which is a belt production-line process. When a production line would break for lunch, the mechanics would break down the movable parts and remove them from the housing. The cleaning crew would bring the rectangular tank on wheels in and clean all the parts, and then the mechanics would return to the area, apply white grease, and reinstall the parts.

This procedure occurred on the five lines, each day, six days a week, sixteen hours a day. Because the cleaning process seemed to be easy and required very little thought and some effort, it would work for me. I also found the service station owner whom I had previously worked for and was able to secure a position servicing vehicles on evenings and weekends. Working both positions offered me the opportunity to see some of the people I had known before being drafted. Sometimes things seemed to be different compared to before the two years of my absence.

Probably because of my past experiences and training, the Campbell Soup position became too slow and boring. After a month or so, I began looking daily at bulletins and the announcement board for other position possibilities. About two weeks later, I noticed a position opening in the quality control Department, so I applied. I also decided to work as often as I could in order to save some money while I was waiting for the college documents to be processed.

The QC personnel had to make sure every ingredient would be included in its assigned mixture, record that addition, and collect the card for that one. Occasionally, a taste test had to be performed. It seemed to me that the QC had more importance than the cleanup crew. Boy, was I ever mistaken. I later realized that the entire operation of this plant was a well-oiled machine in itself. However, the position did pay more per hour.

Every person had a specific job to do at a particular time to ensure the machinery and human factors worked in harmony. If one failed to function properly, the entire production line would be shut down. From properly cooking the meat at the right temperature down the line to the finished product being packaged and quick frozen and cased, the entire operation itself was a well-oiled machine.

About the third month after our return from military duty, my new bride's cousin opted to have an open house/welcome home party on a Saturday evening. I came home after work, changed clothes, and went to join the party. I had expected to have dinner before going off to a party. For a nondrinker as I am, this party was not going to be interesting. There were only chips and dips for food, and there seemed to be a large variety of hard liquors.

To be sociable and meet new people, I began drinking a beer and roamed. As the beer began to get low, the cousin brought a strong mixed drink and proposed a toast. Of course, the mixed drink seemed to tickle my taste buds as it teasingly flowed over my hungry but confused tongue and into my empty stomach. Back at the snack table, someone mixed some drinks using slow gin as I gathered a plate of chips. The slow gin seemed to slow me down a lot.

Because I'd had no dinner or solid food to eat before or during the party, it wasn't too much longer until I started feeling warmer and smooth. After about three hours, we left the party in an attempt to find our apartment. As I drove, I think toward our apartment, I don't remember seeing anything or arriving. However, I do very clearly remember the next morning and the rest of the day how the bed became very uncomfortable as I tested it all day long. On Monday when I went back to work, I knew that I would never force myself to experience the drunken stupor again. And I haven't to this day.

Something was still missing in Modesto. There was no more cruising and seeing friends on the strips. It seems that restrictions had been placed on main street cruising; George

Lucas was gone, and I didn't know where to search for the guys I used to hang out with. I didn't know where to go in town anymore. Through this disillusionment and frustration, I chose to stay true to what I had told the lieutenant colonel and my own drives.

In the spring of 1970, I began the application process of admittance to Fresno State College. My oldest sister and older brother were living in Fresno, which made the application process for residency and financial aid somewhat easier for me.

With my acceptance and financial aid in place and some money saved, my wife and I became Fresno bound. Fresno is about an hour and a half south of Modesto, which meant we were close enough for a weekend visit with our families, or when my wife became homesick, she could make a day trip. We located an apartment about six miles south of the college and settled into a new life and new location. We both found jobs and worked full time. In September 1970, after being able to transfer my credits from Modesto Junior College, I began attending classes.

I found that the closeness or brotherhood I had experienced as a combat soldier in Vietnam could also be found as a criminology major at this college. During the course of attending each class, I had an opportunity to meet and study with various experience levels of fellow students. Between the studying and class hours that were required and working full time, I did not have much time to be balanced with family. As we dealt with each situation as it arose, it seemed that the inflammation in our marriage and relationship began to develop.

As the end of the first year approached, living a new life and in a new city took a toll. My wife had strong desires to have a baby. I believe that she thought a baby would relieve some of the friction and inflammation and fix everything. After a couple months of deliberation, a decision was finally made. I wasn't sure if the time was right or if it is ever the right time. As a male usually thinks, a baby would put a strain on finances until the life goal was met and we were both ready to start a family. A no-frills lifestyle would drastically change. So, in January 1972, we welcomed our son and named him Sean Christopher. He was very healthy and brought much joy to us. His arrival did put a strain on finances and school, but he sure made the extra strain well worth the struggle.

During one of my classes, I became friends with Sandy; we shared the same major and met in one of our psychology classes. It so happened that she was writing her term paper on the same topic as I was: effects of social welfare on modern-day society.

As the months passed by, I decided to change my paper's topic to effects of social welfare on families and children, because it appeared that the directions of both our papers would be the same. Because I was more interested in families and children, I chose to change my topic and direction of my paper.

One day on my way home from school after Sean was born, I saw the classmate who lived across the street. I stopped to tell her about the change so she would feel more comfortable writing her term paper on her topic. I also invited her and a female companion to come over to visit and see our baby.

Needless to say, after my wife saw me talking to the two women but did not overhear the conversation, she became very upset and would not listen to my explanation. I tried to explain to her what went on, but she was unable to hear my explanation. I went to work that evening without dinner. When I returned home after work at about midnight and was getting undressed, I found that all of my T-shirts and underwear except what I had on were all ripped up and torn in half. What else could I do? While trying to maintain a calm demeanor, I told her just how stupid that event was. Now, I had to purchase more clothes, which caused a little more stress on our school finances.

After that episode, I began to notice a pattern of behavior similar to temper tantrums and feelings of being insecure. Though she reacted similarly to all situations during this period of restlessness and adjustment, I continued working and attending classes. A promise kept, I obtained a position as an EOP (Equal Opportunity Program) counselor about November 1971. The federally funded position afforded an increase in pay with a small benefit package. I hoped that the change would rectify the intense situation.

Sean became an active member of our family in January 1972. One day in May 1972, when he was five months old, I went to work as usual. I worked my school facility area, completed my reports and recommendations, and arrived at the house we were renting at about five o'clock that evening.

When I walked through the front door, I had an uneasy-type feeling that our house had been burglarized. As I searched from one room to another, I noticed that in each room there was something out of place or missing. Even my wife and five-month-old were gone.

I called our close friends first, then our acquaintances, and lastly the beauty shop where she worked. Strangely, nobody I called had seen her since the day before. Being confused about finding the house almost empty of linens and clothing, I started to call the Fresno Police to report a possible apartment burglary or worse, a missing person. Just before making the call, I decided to call her parents in Modesto to find out if they had heard from her.

My mother-in-law answered the phone and stated that

she and the baby were there with her. I recall asking her, "Why is she in Modesto?" I was very confused and needed to understand the mystery. When I was told that my wife was going to file for a separation, I was devastated. I had not done anything that would warrant her evasive action. A few years later, I discovered that because of my outgoing personality and post-traumatic stress disorder symptoms I exhibited, she must have had the feeling that I was being unfaithful. I later found out that is exactly what she thought.

One year after entering Fresno State College, my oldest brother, Fred, had purchased a 1969 Corvette and needed to sell the 1964 Corvette Coupe that he had purchased a year or so earlier. Of course, just being discharged from the military and attending Fresno State College with a five-month-old son whom I was now going to support, he had to know that I would not be able to afford anything. But, my brother asked me to buy it from him. He already had the plans on how it would happen. At the time, he knew that I was and still crazy about Corvettes. We reached an agreement after some discussion. His plan was that I could make each payment with the amount that I could afford.

I had to sell a 1968 Honda 350 Scrambler motorcycle, and I was on my way having my very own, first Corvette. I still have that stock Corvette today. So when my wife unexpectedly left, she took the 1967 Chevy Chevelle that we had purchased and drove it to New Jersey. I was left with the Corvette and my clothes and still attending classes at Fresno State College. Needless to say, a divorce quickly followed. I was awarded visiting rights on alternating weekends, child support, and one year of spousal support. There were many weekends that I was not able to have my visits when scheduled. I was always told that he was visiting someone else or sick. Through all these confused times, I was still able to keep my focus on the educational goal of graduating the bachelor's degree program in criminology.

Like most others' situations, many of the events that were ordered by the presiding court were not complied with when my visiting weekends occurred. I then felt that many of the events that occurred were an attempt to distract me from the education goal.

Chapter 11

In 1973, one year before I completed the requirements to graduate, I was awoken at about one o'clock in the morning, after working a double shift at American Safety Equipment Corporation making automobile seat belts. My friend told me that my dad had died. As it turned out, my oldest sister, June, had been trying to call to tell me also. I was just too tired to answer my calls. But I do wish I would have answered that one call. After making an attempt to sleep, I finally got out of bed and got ready to face this day.

I stopped by the ASE office and reported that I wouldn't be in. After driving the hour and a half to Ceres, I found most of my large family at my parents' mobile home. Everyone seemed to be saddened except, guess who—the rock of our family, my mom. She always said that she had to be strong for her kids, who were all adults but still her kids. Incidences as this will create in a person's mind confusion, doubt, and uncertainty, as it sure did mine. My dad would never see or maybe know that his second son did, in fact, complete a college course and graduated.

I also felt I was suddenly an orphan. Being without a father wasn't going to be good. I had worked beside him during my teen years out in the fields. I didn't feel that I was close enough to him besides. I wondered how my mom would get by. Who would take care of her? Many mixed and confused thoughts danced in and out of my feelings. As families will, everyone was offering help to each other. Still, the family rock was solid.

Although my dad's passing was an unexpected shock to all of the family, our lives had to go forward. I had been taught how to stand on my own and attempt to complete whatever I started. So I knew that I had to move forward and complete what I started. The last year of classes moved forward also.

The death of my dad, as expected, became a temporary slowdown for me in work and school. As throughout my life to now, and as in Vietnam, I had to refocus and realize that I had seen death and faced death. My dad would have wanted each of his offspring to move on with life. I did move on with classes, work, and abiding to the court's decision of the year past.

Finally, in June 1974, I was completely finished with my degree. Because I had gone through five previous graduations dating back to the eighth grade at Empire Elementary, I opted not to participate in the graduation ceremonies. As for the four other ceremonies, I knew that no family would attend this most important one.

Very soon after graduating from Fresno State with a degree in criminology, I wanted to get a job that was related to my major. I wanted to get at least some related experience, which I'm sure would look good on my résumé and improve my knowledge. I found my first job after college in the *Fresno Bee* help-wanted ads. It seemed that a retired deputy sheriff had started a security company and acquired a contract to provide twenty-four-hour security at the Dell Webb Building in downtown Fresno.

Trying to get some experience in my field of study, a position as this one would be related directly to my field of interest. I called about the ad and was interviewed the same day. The owner of the company, Aubrey Carter, seemed to be very no-nonsense and to the point. I could respect that and be happy to work for the company. Being a single person with a Corvette, I, of course, chose the swing shift was from three o'clock in the afternoon to eleven o'clock at night. I told Mr. Carter that I would be willing to work at other contract sites if he needed someone to fill in for another person.

My offer was answered about a month or so after beginning the Dell Webb Towne House accounts. One of the graveyard shift officers at Sierra Wine Corporation in Visalia was "sick" and was not going to be able to make it to work. Mr. Carter said he would pay my gas to the wine company site and pay for the hour drive down to the winery. Because I was into making money and serving the security company, I was very excited about the extra work. Besides, I had nothing else to do anyway.

During the course of my employment, I made the trip to Sierra Winery about six times. During my tenure with Carter Security, the local Fresno Catholic Hospital was using off-duty Fresno police officers to provide security in its emergency room, as well throughout the floors and around the grounds. I assume to cut expenditures, the administrator and the supervisory sister decided to maintain the police security into the emergency room and have a less-expensive source of security for parking lots and grounds. They opted to use a contract company to fill the needs of the hospital. When the hospital administrator called Carter Security, Mr. Carter called me into his office before my three-to-eleven shift and offered the position to me. I was a little shocked with surprise and honor that he asked me instead of any of the officers in his employment. When I asked, he said that the hospital wanted a person who was responsible, dependable, and had some college. He knew I had a degree and thought I would be the best man for their needs.

I accepted his offer not knowing where the opportunity would take me or if the position would even work out and be successful while being related to the field of my training. As I did my job, I made notes on everything unusual or out of place. I had to write a report on occurrences on my work shift, which was days, as well as all incidents. I also assisted the police officers in the emergency room when needed. I was really excited about this position. Even the maintenance personnel told me if they ever saw anything that was unusual or needed to be reported. The hospital staff were very helpful.

Everyone in the city of Fresno at the time knew that St. Agnes Hospital was building a new facility on Herndon Avenue, north of the city. The discussion that occurred between the hospital's administrator, the Fresno City Planning Department, and Fresno City officials was on the news almost weekly. It seems that the Fresno City Planners had different ideas than the administrators about where they thought the new site should be located. Then, as now, Fresno City was trying to revitalize the downtown area and knew that if the hospital would move the facility to the downtown area, new businesses of all kinds would relocate to the downtown area also.

It would surely be like giving the city a transfusion of life. However, the hospital administration staff felt that because Fresno already had an adequate hospital near the downtown area, the two would be overkill for the city if both hospitals were located near the downtown areas. The land area on Herndon Avenue was way out in the country on a two-lane, seldom-traveled road. However, it was the final choice for the hospital's new location.

Because the sisters of their order had help from a higher power, the hospital was built on the land with the road seldom traveled. In the early spring of 1975, the new facility was ready to receive its patients. The moving and relocation of equipment and patients with various health issues was a huge undertaking. It was the biggest and most exciting thing that had happened in Fresno in the health field ever.

The residents of the city and county were cooperative and understanding as the special modified buses and ambulances were loaded and made the twelve-mile journey. As they headed northward to the new state-of-the-art facility, along every mile of the synchronized route, the intersections were controlled by a coordinated effort involving the California Highway Patrol, Fresno County Sheriff's Department, Fresno Police Department, and the Fresno Fire Department. My responsibility during the gigantic operation was to coordinate the local traffic coming to the old facility and leaving.

This movement of the entire hospital was completed in about eight hours. This efficiency was partly due to the evaluation and release of many patients who could be sent home and returned to in-home care for their continued care. This entire day was so exciting and busy that I almost did not want it to end. The rush of activities to and from and the excitement of knowing that I was playing a major part of something so huge and so needed was almost overwhelming. Beside the success of the move, a second good thing about the facility was that the administrator offered me an employment position as chief of security.

I was really overwhelmed now. Of course, I sure wasn't going to reject an offer that included a raise in salary, a day shift, and limited job security. Using my abilities that were handed down from ancestors, polished by the military, and refined by education and experience, I began organizing and developing a department of security. First came an office and then came designing my uniform, which was followed closely with a form for reporting incidents that would eventually occur on the facility's campus. Also needed were the procedures for handling any complaints and issues that would arise.

The position I held began with me being the only employee assigned to the new security department. The sixteen hours that I was not on duty were covered by a contract company just as Carter Security had been with Del Webb and the Sierra Wine Corporation. During my employment with the hospital, I had the opportunity to meet a lot of people and attend various meetings, one of which was concerning the projected growth of the soon-to-be medical center. For some unknown reason at the time, I became slightly bored with the position, but I continued to be thorough and do the best job I could.

One of the meetings I was able to attend was a discussion about the proposed growth and the movement of various employee positions to accommodate and balance the growth and needs of the hospital to serve Fresno and the surrounding communities. All information sounded great to me, and I thought that my security department would now be able to expand and develop into the department that could fully blanket its protection and service over the entire campus complex.

To my dismay, about eighteen months after establishing the security department and allowing me to set up protocol and procedures, I met with the administrator. I was notified that the security chief position was being eliminated due to a decision that the hospital wanted to obtain a contract company to provide the entire twenty-four hours of security. What a shocker.

After I picked myself up and dusted myself off, I took a deep breath and readied myself for the completion of a job search once again. I knew that Carter Security, my former employer, had a contract with the Fresno IRS Processing Center. Guess who my first call was to. When I talked to Mr. Carter, he said that he did need two or three more officers for the IRS Center, and I was hired.

I reported to the security guard post at the main gate and was escorted inside where I met Mr. Carter and the lieutenant in charge of the day shift. They both showed me around the massive facility and introduced me to the security officer at each security post. The two things that I noticed about each officer I met was they were wearing logo blazers and slacks and a snub-nosed .38-caliber revolver, which meant that instead of wearing a military-type uniform, the officers were in plain clothes.

The position of security at the IRS was rewarding in many ways for me. The experience and knowledge I gained was unmeasurable. After I had been on staff for almost seven months, one evening while I worked the swing shift, a Fresno city policeman friend named Dennis stopped by for a short visit

He parked the patrol car close to the security post for visibility; however, to my amazement, many of the IRS employees who were arriving for work as, well as those returning after their lunch breaks, began calling the security dispatcher and asking the sergeant and lieutenant if anything was wrong or what was happening.

The officer's visit was unknown to supervisors because it was not an official visit. It was a friend on duty visiting a friend on duty. It wasn't ten or so minutes after our visit began before we were interrupted when I heard a voice on the handheld radio asking me if everything was secure at my area. Dennis and I both knew what the call would mean.

What the call did mean was very shortly the shift sergeant called me on the landline, the telephone system that was being used by each security post at the time. The shift supervisor asked me what was going on. I told him that a friend stopped by to visit for a few minutes. He told me to ask the police officer to leave. Many of the IRS employees were uncomfortable with him being out there. Many others wanted to know if something had happened. I told the voice on the other end of the phone that only those with a guilty conscious would be nervous about his visit. Dennis seemed to understand when I told him what transpired. After Dennis's departure, things calmed down, and the boring duties of the shift continued.

Even though I really did enjoy working at the IRS as a security officer in many ways, my interests were not to stay there forever. While in the position of a security guard at the IRS, I met and became friends with a female officer who was very adept in public relations and knowledgeable with handling a situation. I admired how she could deal with the wide array of situations in an effective manner.

Wouldn't you know it, a couple of years later she later became my aunt when I married her niece. Four years after my divorce, her niece became my second wife. During the time I was employed for Carter Security and working at the IRS, I was notified by Fresno County Sheriff Department to come in for an interview for a position that was open. Shortly after graduating from California State University, Fresno, I had applications pending in every county in California for deputy sheriff and deputy probation officer, as well as a few other positions of interest and had taken and passed the entrance exams for. This was also true for the State of California.

Needless to say, after this long wait, I was surprised when the county of my residence was the first to respond to my interest. My first meeting was with an interviewer from the sheriff's department personnel, and I completed the required forms. Soon after passing a background check, being fingerprinted, and taking an oath, I was sworn in along with a few other recruits.

The men with experience or lateral transfers from other agencies to Fresno County were immediately placed in the patrol units. The three of us who had not yet reached the level and training required for a patrol unit were assigned to the corrections unit. We were all assigned to the graveyard shift, which was from eleven o'clock at night to seven o'clock in the morning. I eventually transferred to the three-to-eleven swing shift because of the difficulty I was having trying to sleep during the day.

After about two years, I found I was becoming more and more unsatisfied and bored with each element of responsibilities of the job. To add to my discontent, when leaving work at eleven thirty one spring evening, a friend and I approached the parking lot where I knew I had parked the Corvette before starting my shift. I did not see any cars in the lot, which was across the street from the jail.

Jim asked me if I was sure that I'd parked the Corvette in this lot. I replied that I hadn't forgotten where I'd parked my car. He accompanied me to the police station to report the carnapping of my car. As the old saying goes, I was fit to be tied, besides being upset.

This was years before my PTSD was diagnosed. The day of the auto theft was Thursday, which was the last day of my work week. I had Fridays and Saturdays off as my weekend. Sometime on late afternoon that Saturday my friend Jim called to tell me that the Corvette had been found in a vineyard on the west side of Fresno County. There was a strong feeling of anxiety, urgency, and anger that engulfed me as Jim told me about the treasure find.

THE NEXT MORNING before reporting for work, I went to find and examine the damaged treasure and to see just how bad any damage was. Here is what I noticed when I found the car: the Holly 650 carburetor was missing, as were all of the water hoses. The fan belt was also missing. I had the vehicle towed to a mechanic shop for further inspection. The inspection revealed a small crack in the rear end support. Later, I found out that the crack could only occur by severe pressure that was caused when the car was racing a Camaro and both cars went over the canal bridge at a high rate of speed. When the Corvette made contact with the surface again, the pressure cause by the weight of the car caused to stress crack. Needless to say, the broken bracket had to be replaced.

After the car had been checked out thoroughly and given clean bill of mechanical health, I took the treasure home and parked it in the garage. The car sat in it protective cave for almost six months before I ever visited the paved road again. I mentioned a little earlier that, I also had an interest in gaining employment with the State of California at the time. I saw the various positions I held as a stepladder to achieve experience and become qualified for a position of higher respect. After taking the state exams, my name was placed on the list of the candidates who were most eligible for the position I'd applied and tested for. I was the third name on the list for the entire state.

I didn't have to wait long. I began receiving cards of interest from almost every department in the state. Each card would have the position title, as well as the department and city or area of position responsibility. A few of the departments that sent me a card were the Board of Equalization; Employment Development, Food and Agriculture; Alcohol and Beverage Control; and Industrial Relations. Of all the state departments, I was most interested in the DMV because of my strong interest in vehicles and the laws related to a vehicle use.

THE SPECIAL INVESTIGATOR 1 position, however, required relocating to Southern California. Upon arriving, I was placed in the Administrative Review Unit. The responsibility of this unit was to oversee and regulate advertising of new and used car dealers to ensure compliance with vehicle code regulations. Additional responsibilities of the administration unit were to perform administration reviews of car dealers' sales book, as well as auto dismantlers' log books. The position required some out of town travel, however. After about four weeks of state employment, I and another new hire were sent to Sacramento to attend the State Investigators Academy. The academy and training were the same academy that was provided to the California Highway Patrol.

However, the investigators did not participate in the driving course. Upon my return from the academy, the supervisor in charge of the local operations changed my responsibilities from the original designation to out-of-state registration. The only difficulty with this change was with the two naval bases in Ventura County. At that time, probably about half of the cars in Ventura County belonged to naval servicemen who were from states other than California.

I had a state car and gas card. With this new designation, came a lot of traveling. Once again, I became somewhat bored. Although being an investigator for the state had been a distant dream job for me, I did become disillusioned with the work assignment change. I believe one of the reasons for the shuffling and reassigning of state personnel was the state budget crisis that California has had for decades.

Even in the early to late eighties, the budget was then never agreed upon and passed for thirty to sixty days. This lack of being responsible caused a rippling effect throughout all state departments, causing reassignments in every department to be done in order to justify a person's position and to show that investigation activities were ongoing.

During this adjustment time, my second wife became restless and uncomfortable being away from her family in Fresno County. I had met a petite woman with a nine-month-old little girl in 1976. We were married in 1978.

Shortly after a garden wedding, I knew that I would want the little girl to be my daughter because a tight bond was created. I wanted to spend free time with her. I could take her shopping or to a playground and do all the things that a dad should do. I had always wanted a son and daughter. I had a son from my first marriage, and now was my chance to have a daughter.

When the baby girl was about two years old, I completed the required forms, filed them with Fresno County Court, and adopted her. My life seemed more complete. As my time as a California State DMV investigator continued, so did my weariness and disillusionment. I began to realize that my dream job was turning into a nightmare. I was becoming stressed to the point that my second wife I were disagreeing on almost everything. Again, something had to change.

One day while getting a haircut, I overheard a customer of the shop talking about how her husband had purchased a retail dairy delivery route from the local dairy, which was selling the local routes. As she continued, she said that he was making more money than he did while working at his previous job. With the discontentment on my heart and mind, I obtained the contact information from her and called the retail route manager. The next day I met with the manager, and he gave me the details on becoming an owner-operator of a business.

With a five hundred-dollar deposit, we completed to agreement and related forms. I turned in a two-week notice of resignation to my former dream job. After the two weeks, I became my own boss and a small-business owner. As I worked and expanded the route, I found that I was more relaxed and actually enjoyed the work. The getting up at three o'clock in the morning was not much fun at first, but I did enjoy being finished with the route loading the truck by about noon each day. I don't believe that my wife really cared whether I worked for the DMV or for myself. Her main concern at the time was to move back to Fresno County to be closer to her family.

After about four months of being a small-business owner and having the flexibility with hours and days of serving, I opted to divide the customers who I delivered to on Wednesdays. With one half I began a Tuesday delivery. With the other half, which was on the outer limits, I delivered on Thursday because I was making deliveries in their area on Thursdays anyway.

The plan that motivated me to even consider a reconstructing of the routes was that by having Wednesdays, off I could volunteer in my daughter's third-grade classroom. The reconstructing of routes and the volunteering proved to be good, I think. The third-grade teacher was a woman who was an excellent instructor in the classroom. She was able to keep control and interest of the students during all phases of her teaching except outside on a field and during what was meant to be exercise time.

When meeting with her, she decided that I could plan and participate in the outside activities, because that was not her favorite thing to do. The planned games and exercising that I scheduled was an easier version of the physical training that I was exposed to in basic training and AIT in the military. Typically, the games were boy teams against girl teams. On alternating Wednesdays, the student who had done well on all phases of classroom behavior and participation would be a captain of the soccer, baseball, dodge ball team, or even track team and be able to choose the persons whom they wanted on their winning team.

This concept seemed to give the students a reason and willingness to strive a little more each day in the classroom, as well as in the outside activities. All the students seemed to enjoy the activities and games. All of the students agreed to our plan when I presented it to them, and they were excited to get started. The teacher said that she even received positive feedback from the parents and school administration about the involvement plan.

As I assisted the teacher each Wednesday, I noticed that something was lacking. It was something that we all have in our lives and some folks can't do without. I remember having a unit or section of study in the classroom at Terra Bella Elementary, Empire Elementary, and Burton Elementary. That segment was what was missing here. When I brought the subject to the attention of the teacher, she said that she didn't know very much about music except to listen to it. That meant that I had some research to do.

Using my investigative skills and desires, I went on the discovery path. Where else to begin but the county library. Keep in mind that this occurred before everybody had their own computer, iPad, and iTunes systems. I began looking for projects that were at the third-grade level and simple to create in a classroom setting. My three main criteria were that the project had to be easy to make, very cost effective or even cheap, and had to make some noise.

The afternoon of the first day of researching, I found what was sure going to be the winning project. I knew that when it was created by their own hands, the children would have a sense of pride and accomplishment because they had created their own. Now that I had found an ideal project, my real work was about to begin.

Knowing that I had access to dairy products and supplies, I began my puzzle by getting the amount that would be needed for each student in the class. Then I gathered about six extra for covering any mishaps that may be made in the creation of our projects. The supply supervisor for the dairy really gave me strange look when I told him that I needed about thirty-five empty paper half-gallon milk containers.

So to keep him from wondering what was going on, I showed him a picture of my idea. He also had a daughter in this third-grade class, so I had to ask him for secrecy about the project. With all of the half-gallon milk containers gathered up, I next set out to find the neck portion of the invention and a roll of line used in stringing a fishing pole or reel. After I found the substance and technique to connect all the parts, I was ready to show the student inventors the project and how we would make it work.

Hopefully, after we built them, the sound would come. The following Wednesday after the outside games, the kids came in and were anxious to get started on their projects. I briefly explained the first step of the project. Each student had to make some room for this operation on his or her desk. I had purchased about fifteen three-inch metal washers from the local hardware store. Using the washers and helping each other, each student cut a three-inch hole in the side of the container facing up (the folded or crimped top of the carton was to their left) and around three inches from where the fold of the carton began. Each inventor affixed the two-and-a-half-inch wide, one-quarter-inch thick piece of crafters' wood to the bottom edge of the container so that the neck (you know that every working and living thing has to have a neck) would extend past the bottom edge of the project. You would have to see it to believe that this skeletal object would actually work and produce sound.

The skeleton project was then set on the counter against the wall with names attached to dry until the next Wednesday. The following Wednesday the kids were so excited they didn't want to go outside for our games. They wanted to work on the mysterious project. Up to this point, I had not told them what the competed project would be.

When we returned to the classroom after the girls had won the game outside, the teacher had them sit in their assigned seats in order to keep order and organization and to contain their excitement. One row at a time was allowed to pick up their skeleton project. When the last row had returned to their seats, I cut one foot off the fishing line for each student. I was very pleased to see the offers to help distribute the line to each desk. When every student had a foot of line material, the next step was to cut a small slit in the carton with the teacher helping with the cutting. After the cuts were completed on the internal fold of the carton, the first piece of line was attached and secured in the slit by tying a small loop or knot and sliding the line into the slit. The opposite end was attached to the extended end of the two-and-a-half-inch neck and tautly affixed.

After the first line was attached and secured, each student had to decide whether he or she wanted three or four more fishing lines on the project. After the installation of the lines, or strings, they were ready for their very own concert. I instructed them to close their eyes and think of their most favorite song ever.

Once this step was completed, their musical concert begun. With twenty-five or thirty milk carton guitars all playing a different tone, all at the same time, one can only guess how enjoyable the guitar concert was to those who had not made one. The amazing musical talent that blossomed during this short concert was definitely encouraged to be continued at home so the family could also enjoy the handmade invention and the "sweet" sound that penetrated the silent air as they listened with patience and endurance.

Needless to say, there were a few words of feedback in response to the rock-and-roll concert that was played at home. This experience, for me, was my first working and teaching kids in a classroom setting and would lead me to do something that I never expected to do. After about a year or so of enjoying the fruits of owning a small business and assisting in the third-grade classroom, my wife decided that she wanted to move closer to her family in Fresno County.

It was after some discussion and choosing between work and my family that a final decision was made. A couple of days later, she packed the sedan with the items she felt she would need to hold her over until I could sell the dairy route and settle all other matters and move also. My wife was going to look for work after she arrived in Fresno. Having to sell the route back to the dairy and receive my deposit was difficult, because I had worked extra hard to add to my customer base, and the route was being very profitable.

It was the experience of the work and ownership in a small retail business that opened my eyes. I was able to see that being of service to the public and providing a product that a person needs or can use while at the same time being honest and fair would be very beneficial. A person's reward would also come.

Earlier I had mentioned that when I had to leave for military service and go overseas, an emptiness and feelings of being unsure of what was to come built up inside of me. Well, having to say good-bye to the class that I had really become attached to and was able to share some fun and knowledge with was that type of difficulty also. I hated to tell the students and teacher of the necessary plans.

But here again it was something that had to be done. As I talked with the teacher while the kids were going to lunch, I noticed that she was becoming a little overwhelmed also. I know that saying good-bye to something and someone is always a hard thing to do, even though I had done it a half-dozen times before.

The relocation and transition back to Fresno County was accompanied by a few difficulties that had to be dealt with before the move could be complete. One such situation was the rental of our house. When we decided to move, after I accepted the DMV position, we rented our house to young single mother. No, it's not exactly what you would probably think. She did take care of the house. But after almost a year, she chose to move. Being in Ventura County, about a five-hour drive south of Fresno County, did create very uncomfortable circumstances. Without a thirty-day notice, she wanted to move immediately. Because my wife had struggled as a single mom, I agreed to allow her out of the rental agreement without any recourse.

The weekend after she notified me, I drove back to Fresno to discuss and settle the financial responsibility with her. While I was back in Fresno, I had to locate another party to rent the house or move back into the house ourselves. It just so happened that the renter and I came to a quick, mutual agreement. We were able to end the rental agreement on a positive note. As soon as the young mother moved out during the next week, I was able to get back into my normal routine. My wife began vacuuming and wiping down everything ready for my arrival in a few days to once again fill the rooms with our items.

Once we were back in our house and waiting for the financial settlement from selling my small delivery business back to the dairy, we began to get settled and start considering what to do to create an income.

I knew that there was and still is a privately owned dairy in Fresno just like the Chase Brothers Dairy in Oxnard whom I had purchased the delivery route from. I knew the son of the founder of Producer's Dairy because we had been members of the same Corvette club based in Fresno in previous years. Because I had gained knowledge and valuable experience in the milk industry and building a profitable route, I felt confident enough to know that I could do the same in Fresno. Because Producer's milk was "Hoppy's favorite," referring to Hopalong Cassidy, a cowboy from yesteryear who was widely enjoyed, I could repeat the building of my milk route empire once again.

I contacted Producer's CEO by phone and set up an appointment. On the day and time of the appointment, Richard and I sat down in his office and talked Corvettes at first to connect me to his personality and concerns. We talked Corvettes because we were both members of Fresno's Corvette Car Club and had the same interests. I handed him a brief and concise résumé that contained all the pertinent information about my knowledge and experience with milk handling, equipment, and personnel care and my interest in being of service to both Producer's Dairy and the residents of Fresno County.

After a brief discussion, he told me that it was funny that I had contacted them and expressed an interest. It seemed that the dairy board of directors had just decided to shuffle some of the dairy's service around and expanded the retail routes. After I told him that I was interested, he said that he would sure let me know when the changes were being made and I could come into the office again to get all the details.

I never did hear back from the dairy's CEO. Because I couldn't and wouldn't sit around and wait for anyone to call me, I had to go out and make something happen. I was told by Chase Brothers Dairy in Oxnard when I sold the delivery route back to them that the reconciliation of the route account would take a few weeks due to the customer payments being on a monthly timetable and the inventory of equipment and supplies. Still waiting for Chase Brothers Dairy, which was beyond my control, I made a decision about Producer's possibilities, which was in my control. I made a decision to call the CEO of Producer's Dairy. I never received a return call or message, so my next step was to contact an employment agency to see what positions that they would have that would match my experience and qualifications.

On a personal note, leaving Fresno for the investigators position caused me to lose contact with many people. Therefore, I had to restart my engine methods. What better place to start but an agency that could actually have information to really help. The agency I contacted had a standard policy of an applicant to come into their office, complete the application process, and have an interview face-to-face with the agent. And that is what I did.

During the interview, she could clearly see that I had experience in dealing with people and also in the dairy cow beverage products. She then asked if I may have an interest in the soda or soft drink industry. I needed a job, so I did.

I was sent out to another interview with the Fresno RC Cola bottler. During that interview, I was asked a series of questions about driving, lifting, counting, and organizing, as well as about my public relations skills. My answers must have been the ones the owner had hoped for. I went to work the next day as a route salesman, calling on grocery stores. I took orders and sold displays of products for each chain store.

This job was similar to the milk route except I wasn't my own boss or in business for myself. However, I did enjoy working for this small bottling company. After about six months of employment with the company, I found out that the entire operation was being financed by the owner's elder retired mom who lived in Santa Barbara. She must have given the son a limited amount of time to turn the bottling company around financially, so it would show a profit.

And that limit on the time was rapidly approaching the deadline. Still, there was no call or messages from Producer's Dairy. So I had to make yet another decision on my job future and chose not to follow up with them, which could have been a mistake. Probably about nine to ten months into working for the independent RC Cola bottler, the financier did unplug all the electricity, shut the machinery down, and force the closure of a small company that produced a very good-tasting soda.

A few years later the 7UP Bottling Company needed a cola in their beverage line of products, and as you probably know, Royal Crown Cola happened to be the one that was purchased. So I was "on the road again," beginning another search for employment.

What a wild transition ride this has become. A good friend who was the in-town Fresno route sales person for a national company that recycled solvents. He called me one evening and told me another route sales position had opened up with this national company that led in its field. As I listened contently, he added that the pay scale was based on a salary plus a commission on product sales. He knew that I had some experience and that I could do well with the company. They were interviewing and taking applications the next day.

What else could we do? Bob and I joined our forces. I found the branch office in Fresno. With the positive attitude that I was the person that Safety-Kleen Corporation needed to hire to help improve its overall service and operations in the Central Valley. Guess what? Bob helped me get hired.

Bob was the Fresno and northern service routes rep, and I was given south counties and southwest Fresno County to service. During the initial interview with the branch manager, I found out some very interesting things about the virtually unheard of company with a strange name.

I was very surprised to hear that Safety-Kleen Corporation was a nationally known company that recycles industrial solvents and cleaners. They provide the service to the auto repair industry and any company that has a need to use a solvent-based product to clean parts or equipment. The federally required documentation is provided by the company, and records of volumes and deliveries are kept for possible future reference. The routes that I was to cover included the rural areas of Tulare and Kern Counties. Both of these south-central California counties are composed of a lot of agriculture land and operations, which meant a lot of driving and real estate between service stops.

At each shop, the machine used to clean parts had a small low-voltage pump that would pump the green cleaning solution up to the cleaning tray. The excess would drain back into the lower portion of the barrel and wait its turn to be delivered up to the cleaning basket again. Every machine had to be cleaned, new solvent solution added, and bag filter replaced. Each red machine had a lid, which could be closed. Each lid had a safety catch in case of a fire. The lid would close automatically. The closing would cut off the oxygen and extinguish the flame. On alternating weeks, one of the routes I had was to the eastern region of Kern County, which is mountainous and encapsulates the high desert city of Ridgecrest, the China Lake Naval Weapons Center, the Indian Wells Center, and Indian Wells Valley.

The service person who had the routes before me must have forgotten to clean any of the red machines. Each one had to be wiped clean. The machines that I inherited were almost crusty with left-on residue. Trip by trip, I exchanged the dirty for clean, and slowly, the desert people and businesses could see that I was interested and concerned about them and their business. This PR was a huge help in selling additional products that I carried.

Many unusual things can and do occur to anyone on the road or traveling. On one of the trips to this high desert area, as I drove the delivery panel truck through the small town, a car pulled up next to me and the driver honked the horn. I looked over to see if something was hanging out of the back of the truck. As I looked over to see what the honking was for, the female on the passenger side raised her top up and flashed her headlights at me. I smiled and waved to them as they sped off. How crazy can people be? I guess it was due to too much California sun.

After I obtained a motel room and went out for food, I remembered when I was investigating for a job with the California DMV that I had to conduct an administration review of a large auto dismantler's records. My Safety-Kleen statement records showed that this business was on my route for servicing. To my surprise, my service stop went well, and I was not recognized. Most service-type routes are usually a routine humdrum, every day, the same old thing. This was pretty much true with a Safety-Kleen route, but because the route I had encompassed a variety of terrain and temperatures during the seasons and changes during the year, almost anything could happen.

Kern County is the largest county in California and is the southern-most county in the Central Valley. Thousands of acres of very rich soil in the farmland is most of the scenery that was first seen by the immigrants who crossed the vast grape vine mountain range after leaving the dust bowl area of Oklahoma and Arkansas in search of a promised land during the late 1930s.

During the much cooler climate that is experienced by anyone crossing through the high deserts of Kern County, a total surprise can arise out of virtually nowhere, resulting in an unsure and insecure feeling of being lost and not really knowing how to search for, much less find, a remedy. The weather conditions can change very quickly and cause a lot of confusion. This happened to me one late fall on my service route to the Mojave Desert area.

I did notice a few dark clouds in the skies. I was to service the equipment Edwards Air Force Base facilities near the small town of Boron. The town of Boron is better known for 20 Mule Team Borax Company. I then had to return to Mojave, which at that time was no more than a wide spot for the junctions of Highways 58 and 14. There are a few restaurants, a gas station, and two or three motels.

Because I lacked cold, icy, and snowy weather driving experience, I was watchful on the ensuing clouds as they congregated and gathered, as in a concert fashion. They seemed to be making plans for a future attack upon the unsuspecting people, who were under their dark and confusing blanket of cover. Most people seem to enjoy the romantic mood and feeling as a gentle, light snowflake makes its way past them on its way to join the ground to end its journey.

But, when there is one, there will be two, then three, then

a dozen, and on into the thousands. While I was servicing the equipment at Edwards Air Force Base, the cloud drifters began to float through the dusk of the evening skies. As I finished and began to exit the base, the large gathering of the thousands of the substance was very noticeable on the road and roadsides in the form of a white blanket, as if to cover and protect the ending of the day.

The dead bushes of the desert as the evening dusk gave way to the dark of the night brought the familiar feeling of the unknown. As I finally approached where Highway 58 used to be, seemed as if the highway must have been moved. Either someone was playing a joke (pranking, as it is to say) on me, or I had not gone far enough from Edwards Gate to reach the highway. Having to somewhat calm myself and focus on the common sense aspects, I kept driving.

There was no traffic coming from or going toward Las Vegas on the white-covered Highway 58 as there usually was, but the road had to be out there. After driving slowly for what seemed to be another seventy-five miles or more (it was actually about three miles), I saw coming from the easterly direction some sort of a bright glare moving slowly in my direction. As I said, out in the high desert, almost anything can happen, and it was slowly coming toward me. I wasn't sure what this bright large glare was or where it was from, but I could see it was coming closer and closer to me. I thought about moving out of the glare's path, but I didn't know which way to go.

Everything covered by the huge white blanket sure looked as if it was all related. As I watched this bright glare, I had to determine whether I wanted to see more or become acquainted as it slowly approached. Finally, I began to see what was causing the glare as it filtered through the thousands of snowflakes that had joined forces to deceive those trying to find their way.

The cause seemed to be at least two of whatever it was. As the unknown approaching glares came more visible through to dampness of the dark, I could see four, which appeared to be bright eyes that looked through the darkness trying to see what lay ahead in wait. As the glaring and moving bright eyes came closer, I could see that to my deliverance, it was a lone diesel truck moving slowly through the maze of snowflakes. I figured that a large vehicle as a semi-truck would first of all see where it was taking its passengers and also probably leave a trail as the huge tires split and spread the snow resulting in a path to follow.

What else could I do? I found out that the windshield wipers worked well as they squeegeed across the two large windows of the van and erased the snow and the blur that was now being thrown on the windshield by the truck's tires. As you might imagine, that day had been a very long and stressful one. But the icing was yet to be put on the travel cake. Once the mysterious glare had passed me by, I was able to find the grooves made by the trucks tires as they attempted to roll over the snow in the road and squished it out to both sides. I only hoped that the driver of the semi-truck knew where he was going, because it seemed that I was going along with him.

Following a truck at about thirty miles per hour through the cold snowy darkness of the night and being overwhelmed with the stress and having to only watch the snowflakes tease as each one made it to its resting place only added to the time that it took to drive the distance to the major desert intersection ahead someplace.

The forty miles that was required to reach the freedom of the intersection seemed to take four hours. Upon finally arriving at the long-awaited destination, the trip had only taken about an hour or so due to how slow we'd moved through the slippery slush. As the lead vehicle successfully approached the dimly lit building of the oasis waiting in the desert snow for our arrival, I could barely see through the foggy haze. The van's lights had a very difficult time locating the drive ramp into what I thought was a parking lot. I decided that I had to stop for the night and rest. I hoped that the storm would be over by the morning.

After parking my vehicle and being able to finally stand on somewhat solid ground, I was able to make my way through the wet, slushy mess that immediately jumped upon my work boots in an attempt to put a deep freeze on my feet and toes, but I was wearing two pairs of thick warming socks that helped keep the warmth in.

I was overjoyed to find a McDonald's restaurant still open for business as the shining and welcoming lights glared through the thickness of the cold, dark night. I quickly tramped through the white mess that was lying in wait for every unexpected person.

After purchasing a "steak dinner," I proceeded through the mucky slush toward the only vacancy sign that I was able to see as the multiple combinations of snowflakes grouped together and floated down to meet their counterparts that landed before they were formed.

As I entered the very welcomed warmth of the motel's office, I found the night clerk asleep on the job. For a few seconds, I flashed back to one dark night in Vietnam when a night guard/sentry who was supposed to be standing watch over our platoon as we attempted to get the much needed rest also fell asleep. I woke up and found him sleeping. That was the first and only time that he slept on his guard watch.

After some thawing out while I flashed back, I tapped the small button on top of the half-dome silver bell that sat on the counter. The clerk told me that he only had one room left. It so happened that the wall heater in the room was not working, but he had extra blankets that I could use.

After about two seconds of careful consideration and evaluating my level of stress and degree of body temperature, I chose to take my cold chances in a room out of the elements with extra blankets rather than sit in an icy, snow-covered delivery van and try to catch some shut-eye sitting in the cold driver's seat. That sure wouldn't work out!

I accepted the extra blankets and was off again through the cold slush that blanketed the cold, freezing asphalt and cement corridors. The close-to-frozen air in the room rushed out to slap me in the face as I opened the door. It seemed to be warning me of this frozen cave to hibernate for the winter's night. As I curled up on the ice-cold bed, I pulled the snow-chilled blankets over my shivering body. I was able to attempt to enjoy the now-cold "steak" sandwich that I'd carried through the cold, over the snow-covered ground, and into the one-man's cave. The time must have been around ten o'clock at night.

After what seemed to be my long winter's nap, I felt very rested and eager to get out on the road once again. The truck's heater would feel really good after the freezing man's cave of the night. After shaving and freshening up, I put my almost-freezing clothes on, tightened the laces on my boots, and outside I went to begin another day. Once outside the man's cave, I saw that there was no light to brighten up the cold darkness of the morning. The snow storm providing the dark blanket now covered the entire area more than ever; it was the blackest cover that I have ever been under. There were no lights of any kind bleeding through the clouds or glowing the promise of warmth. As it usually does during a storm in the desert, the clouds slightly separated as the storm clouds slowly drifted over the land that lay in their path. As I checked the frozen vehicle for safety, I was allowed the engine to warm up, which would provide at least some heat for me to remain in a semi-thawed state while I was driving over the mountain summit.

I was hungry as a bear for breakfast after my long winter's nap. I noticed that the McDonald's employees were not at work yet, probably because of the amount of snow everyone was able to sleep in a little longer, I supposed. I was not aware of the early morning time, but I thought I would proceed on over the summit of the Mojave area, find a restaurant, and have breakfast. I did think it was unusual for a restaurant to not be open for serving food at what I thought was about six o'clock in the morning.

I backed the delivery van out of the space I had parked in the night before, although I could not see the dividing lines that marked each space. As I was met by Highway 58, I continued my trip. I was only allowed to drive about a half mile toward my day's destination and had to stop again at the blocked traffic signal that was then at the location where Highway 14 is joined with Highway 58.

There were three semi-trucks also stopped at the blocked intersection. After sitting and wondering what was going on so early in the morning, my thoughts were of a possible accident on the four thousand-foot top of the range or maybe a malfunction of the signal light. About fifteen minutes slipped by before I decided that I couldn't sit there with the truck still running all day, so I turned the engine off and stepped out to ask the neighbor trucker if he knew the cause for the delay when there were no cars or other vehicles on the road with the four of us.

My stranded neighbor told me that the summit had been closed due to the snow storm that was passing over at the time. Because I had little to no experience dealing with, much less driving in, the snow, especially at night or early in the morning, I would have to sit and wait also. I never considered that the summit of a mountain pass would have had more snow than the lower deserts and be closed. How could they do such a thing on a cold night like this?

It seemed that the California Highway Patrol was escorting the traffic over the mountain pass by using one lane, which had been cleared of enough for a line of vehicles to slowly drive on. After almost three hours of a chilly freeze just sitting in the middle of the freeway and waiting for a turn to be able to encounter the snowy slush and mud of the mountain road ahead, we finally saw a set of lights reflecting through the cold haze. As the reflection got closer to us, we could see that it was our CHP escort, and it was about time!

We were escorted through the thick snow and slippery mud very slowly, as if we were a band of crawling slugs making our way over the mountain to our destination. About an hour later, all of the crawlers finally made it over the summit. Once I was over the snow-covered peak of the ridge, I was able to see the patrol officer make his turn to escort the line of snow-covered cars waiting to see the opposite side of the mountain.

I could have sure told them what was waiting on the other side. When the escort began his easterly journey back over the hill, the crawling slugs were given freedom to continue our journey. Going down the ridge didn't seem to be as dangerous after the California State Department of Transportation vehicles had moved the snow off the asphalt and to the roadsides. As I came closer to the bottom of the ridge and the white cotton puffs began to become more level, I could see what appeared to be lights glistening through the dark and white cold. I hoped they were coming from a warm, heated restaurant.

As the truck slowly crawled closer to the lights, I said, "Thank God." It was a restaurant, and I knew that it would be warm and have hot food. I pulled into the snow-covered parking spaces and stopped. I slowly eased out of the van so I wouldn't slip and fall down and made my way to the glass entry doors that seemed to be heat reflective as I walked closer. I walked inside, found a stool at the counter, and seated myself.

While giving my breakfast order to the waitress, I asked her if the restaurant opened twenty-four hours because it was a quick-thawing warm. The waitress wrote down my order, and as she poured a welcomed cup of steaming hot coffee, she told me that they had just opened at five o'clock. *Five o'clock in the morning?* I thought. *What is she talking about?* I had been up sitting in the snow and thought I was going to freeze for at least four hours, and she tells me that they just opened at five o'clock.

Doubting her about the time, I checked my watch. I figured there wasn't much light that morning due to the mass of black caused by the storming and dark clouds that had lured over us all night long and engulfed us with its freezing-cold temperatures. I had to also check to make sure that the time piece that I treasured was still ticking. To my surprise, it was, and the hands were pointing down. Being tired and cold, it appeared that the big hand was halfway between the five and the six and seemed to be trying to hide the small hand, which was hidden under the larger hand. It seemed that since I'd stopped to hibernate at about ten o'clock the night before and had to wait in the cold snow for three hours before arriving at the restaurant at five thirty, I must have gotten about three hours of sleep. Don't forget, I had a cold burger to eat also.

I stayed as long as I dared, which was about two hours to allow a thawing out. I enjoyed the warmth of the building and the nourishment of the delicious food. While I drank the tongue-burning coffee, I asked the waitress if she thought that any of the local businesses would be opened because of the amount of snow that had turned the entire area white. She told me that usually when the temperatures are as cold as they were plus receiving the six inches of the white covering, there would not be any businesses open in this small desert town.

I finished the delicious, hot food and found my way back to the delivery truck. As I waited for the engine to once again warm up so I could direct the warm air that would soon be coming from the heater toward the driver's seat, I began to contemplate my delivery and service options since there were no businesses open that I could service. I backed out of the space and slowly began to exit the parking lot and maneuver down the empty, cold, and slippery street to see for myself if any businesses that I was to service and clean their machines were open.

They usually opened by eight o'clock in the morning, and it was now eight thirty. While being partially frozen still, I proceeded to drive down the main street of the small desert town and across the white, cold blanket and did not see any business open. Being discouraged and still trying to get thawed out in addition to being tired from the stress and lack of sleep the night before, I made the decision to call the Safety-Kleen office in Fresno to report the disaster of the day and to get the okay to proceed on to Bakersfield where it would be very cool but without the thick white flakes on the ground.

Upon arriving in Bakersfield after an hour and a half of a very scenic drive, I met another SK route salesman who needed some help servicing his route for that day. He shared about six of his customers, and away we went on our separate directions. When the services were completed, I became Fresno bound. When I arrived at the SK yard, I unloaded the empty barrels and loaded full ones along with the miscellaneous cleaners, soaps, and lubricants that I needed for the next day, assuming my thaw would be completed.

As my readjustment back into civilian life continued, I noticed that after about one year of servicing the SK route customers, I began to become discouraged because of the sales restrictions and other requirements that were going to be placed on every route salesman. A few of the requirements were: increase volume sales, which meant to sell more hand cleaners and penetrants, floor cleaners, etc., as well as clean more machines and sell more miscellaneous items at every service stop. It may be noted that very few machines had been cleaned as required on most of the service stops. This was probably due to time restraints and length of each route. There seemed to be a lack of consideration regarding who had the longer, out-of-town routes that required more driving time. We were told to increase our sales, but yet, we still clean the crusty machines.

Although I did my routes as required, which didn't leave much time remaining to sell any of the multiple miscellaneous items, working for Safety-Kleen was enjoyable and educational. I learned processes that a person not in this field of service would never know. That is, learning the legal and federal requirements for the record keeping for chemical recycling.

One of the things I do realize about myself through all of the employment positions I have had, the various experiences that I obtained, and the people I have met is that while working down the many roads of doubt, deceit, and soiled friendship, I do enjoy working with people and serving them.

Reflecting back into the past on my work habits and the positions that I have held, I recall a few years, back to 1979, my brother-in-law Steve was working for his uncle in a business of painting, which included both residential and commercial structures. Steve and I were married to sisters. Through the family relationship, we became close friends. Then and up to now, Steve has almost always done what is commonly referred to in the trades as a side job. A job on the side is usually a small job that can be done after regular working responsibilities and hours or a job that could be done on a weekend and would not interfere with a person's regular job and its hours.

I was aware that Steve and a couple of his friends were doing side jobs to make extra money. I began asking him if I could help with doing anything at all. I knew that there wasn't much difficulty putting paint on a wall. I knew that it would stick to whatever surface it was applied to. Little did I know just how difficult painting would be. I always got the answer back from Steve that he didn't need any help. I repeated my request for about a year. I guess he became very irritated with the constant asking and irritation. I suppose it was the same feeling almost every parent experiences from a bored child asking about five miles down the road after leaving their driveway if they are there yet.

After a year or so, and I knew it was to put an end to the sixty-four questions, he agreed to let me help him and his small crew on a weekend job. He thought it would be a job that he would be able to watch and make a determination on what little ability, if any, I had. That decision began a long-term relationship in the construction field as well as a lifelong, very close friendship with Steve.

A few years after marrying his high-school sweetheart, Steve and I are very close and have a strong bond that would hold our friendship together as Gorilla Glue holds things. We remain brothers-in-law through the thick and thin situations that life would hand us. Steve saw very early on while helping his crew that I was the one who needed to be helped, while all the time trying to help him out on a side job.

He was always patient while I was in my learning stage of the construction education. Boy, am I very glad that he was. Apparently, his uncle was presented with a contract from a permanent, very reputable home builder in the Fresno County area, and it seemed that more help was needed to paint and finish the 2,500- to 3,500-square-foot homes.

I felt I knew how to paint, and I was ready to get started with this bigger adventure. Needless to say, I knew very little about the proper way to prepare and finish any phase or segment of a production type of painting and finishing. Here again my old friend took extra time to teach me how to properly prepare an item or area to be finished. The preparation phase was not really what I hired on for. I wanted to spread and apply the paint and the colors. I learned my lesson the hard way and discovered that I had to set aside my ego and realize that every good job needed to be prepared the correct way.

Once I finally learned, each house we completed brought us joy and a self-satisfaction that the job was done completely and the overall look was very pleasing. From those days up to today, as Steve and I work together, we are like a well-oiled and synchronized machine. One gear knows exactly when the other one will need something done and get it done before the event will be needed.

These lessons have brought the experience which have strongly built my confidence in doing a job well after others seemingly work hard to destroy it. With the renewed confidence and the experience that I had, my relationship with others and working for them began to shine.

After about thirteen years of marriage, I noticed a division being drawn between the marriage vows and causing a wedging effect that began to grind away at the small amount of happiness to I was holding on to. My wife seemed to be getting restless. She began going out with friends and dancing. The progression of the behavior eventually led to her staying out all night on a few occasions. This meant that our daughter and I were not a part of her life as I thought. However, I have always told my partners that if they ever found another person who they would rather have or be with, I would want them to let me know instead of sneaking around behind my back.

My wife agreed to the suggestion, and the days continued on. Each day I began to become more aware of the jagged and roughness of the unwelcomed wedge, as it worked its way between us. After all, up to this point, we had been involved with keeping fit by conducting workout sessions synchronized to music as aerobics and dance some gym workouts and running races. Our daughter was also very active in both soccer and basketball during the better years. Although we did have our struggles, we seemed to get past them. We both worked hard in order to maintain the financial responsibilities that we agreed to.

Sometime during the fourteenth year of our marriage, the rocks began to slip and move and get bigger and rougher. We had some difficulties trying to maintain the straight and smooth road we'd been on years earlier. I believe all this was caused by many things, including my struggle with PTSD and working some long hours in order to maintain a comfortable lifestyle. A second possibility would be that because I was not our daughter's biological father, much of my disciplinary authority was overruled.

The rough edges of the wedge had done severe damage. Somehow I knew that she had used up all of the love and compassion and wanted to be released from her marriage vows.

She did tell me that she didn't want to be married any longer as we had agreed years before. The rope had come to its end. Of course, a divorce was applied for and became final on the day of our fifteenth anniversary. Not knowing at the time about post-traumatic stress disorder and that I did have the disorder, I knew that I had to force myself to stay calm and collected in order to deal with everything that was going to be coming toward me in the years to come.

Chapter 12

I could become irate and start drinking heavily or something worse if I would have allowed the control patterns of PTSD. That, however, would then be viewed by many as the reason why the terrible wedge was driven deep. After emotions of the situation calmed and I was settling into a single lifestyle once again, I had to find something I could do to keep my mind occupied and myself busy while I rebuilt my self-esteem. Having the '64 Corvette, I decided to join Central Valley Corvettes of Fresno and became active as a founding member.

The club began in the late 1990s when about twenty or so enthusiasts decided to branch off from the original Fresno Corvette Car Club and start a club with less controversy and stress. I chose to move on with my life and enjoy Corvettes and be with others with the same interests and had no intention at the time to be involved with anyone but the club.

There were a few good friends, like Chuck and Susie Vencill, as well as Terry and Donna Caparso, who thought differently; however, it seemed that many of the members knew someone who was looking for someone who wanted to meet someone to spend time with and accompany her on the Corvette runs and outings.

About six months slipped by when Terry and Donna, former presidents of the club, introduced me to a woman who wasn't looking for someone either. I seemed to be a little pressured to ask her to the club's dinner run the next weekend. When I asked her, she told me that she was busy. I felt somewhat relieved, though, as I now had a choice to either attend or stay home. A few days later I received a call from the woman. It seemed that her plans had been changed, and she wanted to let me know that she would like to go to the dinner if the invitation was still open. I found out later that Donna had called and talked to Sue, because she really didn't any have plans for that weekend.

Sue worked with Terry at the local AT&T office. It so happened that Sue was originally from Connecticut and moved to Fresno to help take care of her parents. She had recently gotten a divorce and thought the change would be good. During the club's patio dinner, we sat and talked to get acquainted. I could tell that she wasn't very interested in much.

A few months later, one of my nieces got married, and we attended her wedding together. During the reception, I had the honor to dance with the mother of the bride (my sister) for the parents' dance. My sister was a widow and couldn't dance by herself, and I wanted her to be able to dance at her daughter's wedding.

While we were dancing, I wondered what our mom was thinking, because we were reared in a church that thought drinking and dancing were sins. Later I asked my mom, and she said that it was good we danced together. Needless to say, Sue and I did continue dating and after about a year or so, we became engaged while at O'Hare International Airport in Chicago.

Here is why I asked her at O'Hare. We were on our way to attend Sue's cousin's wedding in Vermont. The proposal came, I believe, because of the upcoming wedding; our feelings seemed, at the time, to be strong, and we were excited about the wedding event. When she hesitated for a minute, I suspected that she wasn't really sure. The engagement lasted about a year. Now, I suppose that I could have been more romantic and chosen a much nicer setting for the question. In August 1994, the engagement was called off. It wasn't because of the setting for the proposal.

I became involved with a global marketing company in about 1989 distributing a very good line of household products, and it was constantly expanding various product lines in order to better serve its distributors as well as their customers. Every three months there was a weekend meeting that ranged from encouraging to introducing new products that would be available sometime in the future months.

One such weekend gathering was being held in St. Paul, Minnesota, in the spring of 1994. Now, if you recall, the story of while I was at Fort Lewis, Washington, in the army's basic training, I left the company area to deliver a couple of items to a friend who was in the air force at the time. On my way back to my company area through a closed company area, I was caught, reported to the CQ office, and was totally chewed out in front of my squad by our company's second lieutenant. Well, that friend whom I risked all for at the time was my high school friend/sister Dottie. Dottie and I always stayed in touch until her death in October 2013.

After Dottie retired from the Air Force, she and her husband, Jon, (who, I am told, is one of Wyatt Earp's great-grandsons) purchased a home in southern Illinois. The couple had been inviting me to visit them for a few years, and they were very aware of my marital situation, as well as the not-so-happy engagement. I had been very open with Dottie because I'd known her as far back as 1961 when she was a freshman in high school and I was a big sophomore. We hung out with the same of friends and quickly became like a brother and sister. Actually, I was closer to her than my own sisters.

We had a closer relationship with each other than we did with our own blood siblings. So why wouldn't we be close? That is why I knew she was stationed at McChord Air Force Base when I was at Fort Lewis. It was easy to stay in touch with her over the years. Our relationship was so good and meant so much that her parents both considered me their second son, and Danny (Dot's only brother) was good with that.

They were aware of my spiritual background. When in 1990, at the death of their dad, Danny and Dottie asked me to perform the funeral ceremony, which included military honors and a six-gun salute. This was my first funeral to conduct, and Dad Dan was like a father figure to me. The proceedings were very difficult to get through.

I almost didn't make it through the proceedings. In 1998, Dottie's mom went to join Dan, and I found that somehow the second funeral came somewhat easier to do even though my relationship with my second mom was closer.

When the three-day event in St. Paul deadline came closer, I called Dot to let her know that I would be in Minnesota. After the events were concluded, it would be a good time for me to come by for a visit. When I called and the call was answered, I thought I had called the wrong number because there was a strange but friendly voice on the answering end. Being former law enforcement, I became concerned and started with the sixty-four questions.

The voice on the other end seemed to be nice and willing to help me out as I asked for my friend, who better still live there if I intended to come for a visit. As our conversation continued, I learned that my phantom friends were out, and she was supposed to be feeding the two dogs and two cats after she managed to get all four back into the house. When I told her who I was and noted that I'd try to stop by for a couple of days when I left St. Paul, she said she had heard my name mentioned.

As I received the warm feedback, I continued asking the sixty-four questions and hoped they weren't coming across as an interview. Today, I cannot recall exactly what we talked about for two hours, but when she told me the animals were inside and probably hungry, we both agreed to stop before the dog fell over and put its four legs up in the air to demonstrate about the late feeding and its hunger.

When my sister/friend and her husband returned from their dinner date, she called me back and told me that she had talked with their roommate, Tanya, who had told her about the strong possibility of a visit. Dot told me that they had been wanting me to come to visit and see their Victorian-style house and their community. The true reason had not yet been revealed, however.

During the conversation with Dot, possible plans were made for my visit. I would fly from Fresno to Denver, changing flights, and then fly on to St. Paul. After the function in Minnesota, I would reroute from St. Paul and fly down to St. Louis where Jon would pick me up. It seemed like a good plan that would surely work out.

While waiting the month and a half for the trip to the Twin Cities for the major function, I felt more compelled to call Dot's number more often than I had in the past years in order to ease or satisfy the unknown desire that was constantly disturbing my emotions. It appeared that Dot and Jon's "roomy" must be in the capacity of a maid, because she seemed to answer the phone about 90 percent of the time I would call. Actually, that was the real reason I did call so often. When my sister Dot would answer, I would create a reason for the call and the reason usually was wrapped around the trip to St. Paul.

I doubt if Dot was as shallow thinking as I gave her credit for. And maybe I was too naïve to know that she knew of my heartfelt desires. One should keep in mind that I had been involved and engaged to Sue for about two or three months when I was to make the trip to the Twin Cities area. Sue had always refused to accompany me on any business trip. My fiancée and I, it seemed, were headed for a fiasco. I could clearly see this but refused in my mind to accept it.

No one wants to be a failure in anything he does, so failing in this relationship would surely be my fourth. (They are: one that began in high school and rekindled in junior college; my first marriage, which ended with her leaving with my five-month-old son; the second marriage, which ended when she became restless; and now this engagement. The fourth seemed to be confronting me now.) The fiasco grew closer and closer as she continued to ignore me and refused to accompany me on any small trips that I felt were needed. Never wanting to spend time together and refusing to have dinner with friends or go on a double date were some of the signs that something was wrong. I also noticed a controlling attitude and wanting to have everything her way. So when the inevitable happened, I wasn't surprised but was ready.

When the date and time arrived for the three-day weekend trip, which was in May 1994, I arrived early and had to wait about two hours. Once on board the plane, I anxiously sat in my assigned seat next to the window. I sure enjoyed seeing the wide view of the earth from thirty thousand feet and watching the clouds as they seemingly rushed by as the plane passed and reached out to find another scene for me to enjoy.

When the airship landed at the Twin Cities airport, I could

tell that my anxiety was almost as big as I was. I had never been to the Twin Cities area before, and I wanted to see just how close these twins were. To my surprise, I found that they were almost joined at the hip. The area around them is almost breathtaking. The family reunion in St. Paul was composed of the many branches of the family tree within the business. They were all brought together to renew, revive, and keep strong the close relationship with others within each family branch. It was also a time to see how each branch responded to the leaders and their trunk of the support for each individual business.

The long weekend was exhausting but yet enjoyable. When the business family reunion was finally over, I was packed and ready to check out of the hotel. After checking out, I didn't waste very much time getting to the airport.

I did not know that the next time the airbus would land, it would be bringing me to one of God's greatest gifts to me. I can't remember how long the flight was from St. Paul, Minnesota, to St. Louis, Missouri, because I more than likely fell asleep. Because Jon and Dot knew the time of my flight arrival, Jon was waiting to meet me and help gather my luggage at the baggage claim area. Jon and I talked a lot about the family reunion weekend, work, and all of the multiple topics that are talked about. The closer we came to their house, the more I found myself getting nervous about arriving. I knew that when we arrived, I would be meeting the sweet, soft, understanding voice that I heard and was drawn to on the phone.

It would be thrilling just to meet the person who had the voice that I enjoyed on the phone. As we pulled into Jon's parking space in the backyard just beyond the white picket fence, we exited the van. Walking through the small garden and with every step down the small dirt path, I looked to see if anyone was going to come out of the house to greet us.

First appeared Dot coming out the back door and down the three or four steps. The last time I'd seen her was in 1990 at the funeral of her/our dad. So to see her coming down the step was a happy site. So there we three stood talking. I asked Dot about their roommate, Tanya. Dot told me that she had taken some vegetables over to her dad's house and should be back in about fifteen minutes. As Dot turned and went back inside to cook dinner for us, Jon and I walked the property as he explained and pointed out things he thought would be of interest to me.

With Jon knowing that I was a handyman, he showed me a few areas where he could use some assistance. The next fifteen or twenty minutes seemed to creep by before we saw a white Dodge turn into the driveway. Jon and I walked toward the driveway to meet and greet and help in any way we could. Jon introduced me to the angelic voice that I had been anxious to meet. After hearing her on the phone, I couldn't help but to think, *So this is her.* As my eyes caught her appearance, I noticed that she seemed to be like a breath of fresh air. She did appear to be a refreshing sight.

I shook hands with her as a person who is already engaged to another should, and she returned with a handshake grip and a large, warm, bright smile. After some small talk, the three of us went inside to offer Dot some help with preparing dinner. She did need some help with almost everything. That's when I found out that my newfound friend just happened to be an excellent cook.

Tanya had brought veggies for a complete salad. Dot prepared the chicken, and Jon and I prepared the bread and table settings. Needless to say, the meal was delicious, especially since I was a bachelor and was returning from a three-day weekend of restaurant meals. The home cooking and friends was the best way to wind down the week.

After dinner, we all crowded in the kitchen area to do our part in cleaning up and doing the dishes. Now we were all ready to sit down to watch a movie and share our stories of when we were in high school and how we each arrived where we were. We all had some funny stories—the ones that were true. The first night I ever spent in my sister's house turned out to be a lot of fun, and we were able to catch up on the goings-on during the past years.

When the storytelling and laughter ended, sometime in the wee hours of the night, I wasn't sure of the sleeping arrangements. I began walking toward the back door, which just so happened to be the door that we'd used to enter the house earlier. Dot broke through the muffled noise of our shuffling as we moved out of the TV room to embarrass me by telling me that they had indoor plumbing and I wouldn't have to go outside.

Trying not to reflect any sign that I was a little embarrassed, I told her that I was going out to sleep in the spare room in the guest house, which was a small, partly finished room across the backyard. Since we were not being funny now, she had me go to the den area to a large sofa that pulled out to transform to a bed.

My earlier experiences with this type of sleeper sofa was mostly received at my mom's mobile home. She had a single bed that had to be shoehorned into this small eighty-by-eight-foot room that she called Jerry's Room, and that is where my man cave was whenever I visited. The reflection of Jerry's man cave must have had some projection, as I must have given Dot a weird or strange look as I recalled my man cave and my uncomfortable sleeping experience.

The silence of my recall was broken when she assured me that the mattress was very fluffy and soft. Being a guest in her house, what could I say? The sofa bed looked very soft, and I doubted I would have much difficulty falling asleep and staying asleep. The four of us sort of roamed around in the kitchen area as if none of us wanted the evening to end or to go to bed. Finally, Tanya broke the mysterious silence and said that she had to go to work the next day and needed to get in bed.

She gave Dot a hug, gave Jon a quick kiss, and came toward me. I could feel the nervous warmth begin to spread over my entire body as she began to close in on my position. Silly things ran through, across, and around my head. Like, *Should I also kiss her? After all, I am engaged to someone else who seemingly never wants to be with me. Do I put my strong arms around her and pull her toward me real tight? Or do I do both? Or should I just give her a small peck on her cheek or on her inviting lips as a friend would do so that she doesn't get the wrong idea or see almost through me.*

After all, I was sure that my sister had told her a lot about me and how I was. I didn't want her to think or feel that I was trying to fill in the blank areas that Dot missed or didn't know anything about. When this well-known stranger was finally standing in front of me, a fast decision had to be made. Well, what would it be? She hesitated only for a moment and cleared my mind of all the "what should I do's" by coming close and giving me a quick, light kiss and saying good night.

I'll tell you, that small, quick peck lingered with me as I finally laid down on the queen-sized sofa bed and all night long. I probably spent the majority of the night lying there awake, thinking and wondering if she was asleep. I fantasized that she was also awake, tossing and turning. Much like the 1980s song, I could still feel her kiss upon my lips. As the darkness and silence of the small town moved through each room of this two-story home, I couldn't help but wonder if she would be able to hear her alarm, if she had one, and if it was set to wake her up.

If the alarm was forgotten before she went to bed, would it be appropriate for me to go to her second-floor bedroom and wake her up or at least make sure she was already up? I wasn't sure if that plan would be the best one, because she might have thought that I had a different motive and wanted to make a move on her. After all, we'd just met that day and really didn't know each other at all.

I might have fallen asleep for an hour or two, but during all the minutes I was awake, many good thoughts and some that were not so good did their little dance across my mind and tickled my senses until the morning dawn light finally cut through the thickness of the dark and forced the dark to surrender.

As the light of this April morning became brighter, I could hear some rustling movement and noise coming from the upstairs bathroom, which was being remodeled. I didn't know at that moment if it was my longtime friend or if it was the one who caused my all-night question session and very few answers. Sometime later, I heard footsteps coming down the stairs.

As I looked up, I saw a lovely, well-dressed woman coming down to the first floor. As her first foot was placed on to the carpet of the small hallway, I could clearly tell that she was wearing a fragrance that once it entered into the nostrils it began to take control of and consume the sense of smell. As the sense of smell was empowered, the engraving into the memory of the tantalizing sweet and unforgettable smell became permanent. To my surprise, my sister/friend Dot must have gotten up earlier.

Although I did not even hear her make any kitchen noises, Dottie met Tanya as she entered the kitchen area with an empty plate in her hand and told her that she would have to help herself with whatever she wanted to eat. I'm not sure if it was because I was sneaking into the kitchen area or because she was running late for work, but she did not eat much of anything. I thought she was eating like a hummingbird.

As a surprise to me, she asked me if I could take her to work. Duh. What could I say? As we drove, she explained to me that Jon wanted me to do some repairs in the construction project in the second-story bathroom. Because he would need his car for his work, I might need a vehicle so I could get parts or materials as needed. How nice of her to offer me her car for the day given the fact that we'd just met the evening before. As things turned out, I needed a car to get materials. I guess she was looking ahead to be helpful.

When she called later in the day, she asked me to meet her after work for a ride home. What an excellent idea. After finally locating her job site and on our drive home, she volunteered another day of loaning me her car. However, the second day came with a small condition attached. After taking her to work again, probably to learn my way around, I could use the car. She also added the condition of bringing her lunch. When I asked her what kind of food was her choice, she replied for me to just bring finger food. So what are finger food items exactly? Remember, I am a guy. Almost all food is finger food. When I asked her what would she prefer, she responded with a slight chuckle and educated me. Finger snack foods, it appeared (I couldn't believe it), were any variety of crackers, sliced or cubed cheese, some veggies, some fruit, and a person always needed something to wash everything down with.

I remember thinking how romantically cool a finger food picnic would be with a new friend. After taking her to work on the second day, I was on my way back to Dot and Jon's house when my mind and imagination began to short-circuit trying to figure out where to take her for a picnic and hope that her choice wouldn't be the company's break room.

Because Dot worked with Tanya, I couldn't call her for any suggestions. I had no knowledge of any park or good place to take her, so I decided to not worry, if I could help it. Won't you guess, the few hours I had that morning were as slow as a snail crawling toward his next meal. My anticipation and anxiety grew more and more, as if a balloon was being blown up and I was waiting for the explosion pop. As the time grew closer, I had to find the food items.

I opened one of the cabinet doors, and the box of wheat crackers seemed to just jump out for me. *Well, that was easy,* I thought. Of course, the cheese and cold-cut items would naturally be found the fridge, but which one? I never did like to look through people's houses or the fridge in search of anything. But because someone was counting on me and my decisions for her lunch, I figured it would be okay to look for the chilled food items that would be tasty and pleasing to her.

When I opened the door of the fridge, I found some great finger food items that were already in a container and just waiting to go. If the grapes were already packed for a luncheon picnic, maybe the other chilled items would be also. As I pulled the first drawer out to expose its contents, I found two blocks of cheese that I could cut and make into cubes.

In the second drawer, I had to move a few food items in order to locate the large chunk of ham that was just sitting there and waiting for a knife to slice through it. I cut and sliced the meat and cheeses, gathered the new box of Wheat Thins, and was ready to go out the door. But wait! I needed something else. Oh yeah, a few veggies, and I also needed something like a basket to carry the luncheon supplies in.

After locating a woven bamboo basket that by chance was sitting next to the dining table, I neatly placed all of the items inside the cloth lining, grabbed a roll of paper towels, and loaded everything in the car. But something was still missing. What could it be? Not able to think of anything else, I started the car and backed out of the driveway. It's funny how a little air can blow the dust and cobwebs out of your mind when it becomes clogged up from the anxiety and nervousness of planning something as important as a first luncheon or first date.

About halfway to my destination, I remembered what it was that I forgot to include. I had to stop and purchase something to wash all of the luncheon down with. Otherwise, we both may need CPR performed or a choking movement done. Somehow, I manage to arrive for the luncheon a few minutes early.

My lunch date must have been anticipating my arrival, because she was ready to elope for an hour when I walk through the door. The trip to the Central City Park was about a ten-minute drive. Upon arriving, Tanya retrieved a colorful blanket from the trunk of the car and spread it out to create a warm, private area that would be ours only as we consumed our goodies. The time for our perfect lunch passed by quickly as we shared and talked about things. We discussed our lives' events and our own journeys, as well as work-related and family-related stories. Very shortly after the colorful blanket was spread out on the green grass, the time had arrived for it to be folded and placed back into the trunk of the car.

Reluctantly, I had to return my eloped partner back to work. We barely made it back on time. Remember the tossing and turning that I mentioned as I tried to find some comfort on the sleeper sofa on the first night? Well, it seemed that Tanya was also turning and tossing on the first night. I'll tell you, I did not know what was going on, and she probably didn't either. It wasn't until I returned to Fresno that I was slapped in the face with a reality that I was completely unprepared for and sure wasn't expecting.

During the late evening, after the darkness completely filled each room and engulfed the house, Tanya and I were sharing our thoughts while we inspected the remodeling of the upper bathroom. As I was preparing to leave and return to the lonely den where the cold sleeper sofa waited for me, I believe it was she who suggested that she had been cold also.

The house used a steam heater system to heat each room. Jon must have turned the steam up on the room heater that night, because it sure was hot and steamy all night long. Somehow, Tanya was able to try to get out of bed while the alarm was going off. I finally allowed her to get out of bed. After using the facility, she began to put on the little makeup that she used and got her hair ready to complete fix. She was finished getting dressed and fixing her hair. She went downstairs, spreading the same wonderful perfume scent that was still in my nostrils and memory from the night before.

As she and Dot talked softly, Dot told her that they should hold the volume down because I was still asleep. Of course, Dot was thinking that I was still resting on the sofa. Tanya told Dottie that I was upstairs and not to worry. Dot, of course, thought that I was in the bathroom already. Realizing what her friend meant, Tanya said that she had a surprised look on her face.

The morning of the third day began as the first two days of my stay. The warming morning sun rose as the darkness of the night made its exit. The big difference with this day was that not only did Dot take Tanya to work, but I was going to use the white Dodge to charter some unknown territory. I had been in touch with Steve Stotler, a fellow First Cavalryman whom I'd served with in Vietnam. Steve lived in Peoria and was an avid golfer. When I returned from my Vietnam duty, I had purchased a 1967 Chevy Chevelle that my first wife and I used to drive across the country on Interstate 80 to Fort Dix, New Jersey. On the way to the Fort Dix destination, we stopped in Peoria and had dinner with Steve and his family. His family is made up of wonderful people, and we were treated like long-lost friends.

Because Steve was an international sales rep for a major tractor company in the Peoria area and was on his way to Europe, he agreed that Springfield would be the best local city for us to meet for brunch. With Jon's freeway directions and Steve's restaurant directions in hand, I set off on this journey into the unknown territory.

Driving north on I-55 toward the state capital of Illinois, it was a sunny and warm day. It was an ideal day for such a drive and to meet with a buddy whom I'd served with for eleven months and hadn't seen for twenty-five years. As the white divided lines passed by, I was able to enjoy the unseen area in which I knew that Pres. Abraham Lincoln had probably traveled in the 1860s. I did notice that the roadsides were uncluttered, and the road surface seemed to be absent of roughness and chuck holes as most of the roads in California are.

It seemed to take almost forever, but I finally saw the road signs alerting me that the street I was to exit on was nearing. As I became closer to the exit, I could tell that my anxiety level began to rise higher than the levels of discovering something new and knowing that President Lincoln was born in this area of our country.

I finally reached the exit with anticipation and made the turn that would lead me to my destination and my old Vietnam buddy. About a block from the interstate exit, the sign for the restaurant came into view. I began to wonder how much he had probably changed since I saw him in late July 1969 when I was on my way to New Jersey.

As I entered the front doors of restaurant, I quickly scanned the entrance to see if Steve was waiting at the front for my arrival. When I didn't see anyone who might even resemble Steve slightly, I had to ask the woman at the wait-to-be-seated sign for help. She said that my friend was waiting and led me to the table where he was squirming with a cup of hot coffee in his fingers and taking a sip of the hot liquid.

As the woman approached the table with me in tow, Steve stood to meet his old buddy. What a thrill it was for both of us to meet, if only for a short time, and to catch up as much as we could. When we were finished with our small brunch meal, we asked the waitress to take a picture of us with the small disposable camera that I had brought with me for just this purpose. After about three pictures were taken of us, it was time to pay our ticket and depart. Steve said that he had to fly to Detroit for business that afternoon, and I had to find my way back to where I'd begun this maze.

One of the highest points in my life as a veteran was to meet with a fellow veteran, even though it was for a short time. Since that meeting, I have been able to contact a few of the guys whom I served with but have yet to meet with them as I did Steve.

The long trip through the return maze to where I began my journey just a few hours earlier turned into a mystery journey of its own. The directions I'd received from Jon the evening before sure looked different on the paper as I began heading south on I-55. The sides of the road had areas that looked familiar. The roadside rest stops all looked the same, even though I had just passed by them a couple of hours before.

Because of the hour of the day, there seemed to be more traffic on the road, and some of the drivers must have thought they were in training for the Indy 500. It couldn't have been because I was taking more time and driving slower than the speed limit. Their driver's training seemed to add to my nervousness as I navigated my way south on the wide-open space of this Illinois interstate.

Probably about halfway through my return trip, I noticed a turn off at Granite City. I do recall seeing a similar sign. I thought I had gone passed my destination's turn, so I took the turn. It wasn't long until I thought, *Oops! I sure don't recognize this area.*

As to not get more lost and add more mileage to Tanya's car, I had to call her to make sure that I was on the route that I should be on. When I heard the sweet, tender voice on the answering end, a soothing, comforting, warm feeling flowed over me, and I somehow knew that I would be able to find my way home. When new directions were given to me, I checked the new with the original and discovered they were the same. Who knew, simple as it was, I followed the clear directions that had been given to me, and the interstate matched the one I had in hand all along.

Therefore, I continued driving south. Still unsure of myself because of the unknown surroundings, I enjoyed the drive because of the beauty and fresh air of the state, which I was not accustomed to in California. I believe that is what made the difference in not being able to follow handwritten directions

As I finally got closer to the St. Louis freeway system, I began to recognize a few of the city names that I saw on the large green road signs. Once I'd seen one or two of the city names, I began to relax a little, and my stress level became lower. When I saw the sign announcing Interstate 70, I then knew that I could begin my driving descent, because I was almost there.

As I pulled into the driveway, I knew that my journey was finally over. I was so glad that Dot had brought Tanya home from work, because I was later arriving than I had anticipated. Once inside the house, I gave a briefing to everyone before we had dinner. They seemed to think it was funny as I told them about my short detour at Granite City.

To my dismay, the next day would be my last with my old friends, as well as my new friend. So for my last day, I had to make it special. I didn't want to leave her with a lasting memory of something that we could have done and failed to do. I again took her to work, and our departure was a little more difficult than the first couple of days. Our lunch for the last day took place at Our Lady of the Shrine complex, which is quite picturesque and a romantic place where there seemed to be a special emphasis on the no-frill, small finger food lunch that we shared together. It was funny how conversation subject matter was of no concern to us.

We just shared, talked, and enjoyed the surrounding scenery. The return to work was a little harder to do but had to be. When I picked her up at work that evening, I knew it would be the last time for me to do so. Driving back, I thought about just continuing to drive with her forever. I had the inner feeling of not letting her go. I wanted to be with her, because she was easy to talk to. She also felt the same.

The evening meal this last night was not the same as the previous evening. There seemed to be a cloud or a fog of uncertainty mixed with a feeling of sadness that overshadowed the four of us during dinner and followed us into the smoky

TV room. I knew that though I had to leave the next morning to return to the old grind of California life, I sure did not want to. The last evening was made very special for me as the mixed and confused feelings between me and the new friend seemed to reach a very high pitch as my feelings became intertwined with her passion.

The emotions and depth of our feelings became entangled so tightly that we were not able to break free until the next morning. We did not feel like having breakfast the next morning. After we shared the water and lather in the shower, we slowly began to put our clothes on, which was opposite from what we both had greatly enjoyed for the few days before.

As she was still getting ready for her day of work, I was placing my luggage in Jon's van and getting ready to travel the lonely road toward Lambert Field (aka St. Louis Air Terminal). After my last good-bye to Dot and Tanya, Jon and I reluctantly got into his van, and we were off to join Interstate 70 westward toward the airport. Wouldn't you know that all the way there all I talked about was Tanya and how much I enjoyed being with her for the few days that we had together.

I am sure that he became bored with my conversation. He must have, because he dialed her at work and let me talk to her for a while. It was so good to hear her voice again before I left the state. As the phone call ended, Jon could tell that I was having a lot of difficulty seeing through the tears that had appeared out of nowhere. It was the same type of feeling that I had experienced a few years earlier when I was on the airplane flying to Fort Lewis to be processed out of the country.

Jon attempted to comfort me as we continued toward the destination. The comfort attempt did not help. After we arrived at the airport, he once again dialed the familiar number so I would have one more chance to hear the comforting voice that

I missed so much. It was hard to believe that I was a fifty-year-old, twice-divorced, educated man having internal feelings like I was a lost puppy looking for its owner. I'll tell you what, I was about to face one of my greatest fears. Jon stayed near until I had to go through the TSA security checkpoints. After completing the security checkpoints, I saw Jon as he turned to leave.

Then I realized that I was alone and had been thrown into a den with complete strangers. After about seventy minutes of sharing the airport with the other passengers, my flight number was finally called. I was both glad and sad. I was glad to go but sad to do so. Once aboard, I found my seat, locked myself in, and was ready to go.

Because of my heritage and obstacles that I have had to overcome, I have never been someone who was not willing to face and confront my fears or something I really dreaded. A short while after the passengers were all on board and packed away, I heard the mighty jet engines begin to whine as they were getting ready to face the runway and the wild-blue yonder head on.

As American Airlines does for a routine, the flight I was on would fly to Dallas/Fort Worth, and I would be matched up with other strangers. From Dallas/Fort Worth, the trip was a four-hour flight back to California. Thank God the flight was uneventful. However, I was, and always am, ready to respond to any threat or disturbance just as my forefathers would have done.

As planned prior to the St. Paul, Minnesota, reunion, after the flight landed smoothly, I was met by a person whom I thought I knew. However, I now had my doubts and didn't want to meet. I did need a ride home. I had to face and confront what had to be. If you recall, many pages ago I made mention that I was engaged to another woman. Well, a change of heart had occurred while I was gone on this trip. Because the relationship with Sue was not even going to be a good one and was totally not working out between us, I was left with many questions unanswered and a feeling of being incomplete.

After I met Tanya, my circle of life seemed to be closed and now completed. So the difficulty I now was confronted with was what to do about the two relationships that I had become entangled in. One was a long-distance situation that I actually wanted because of the love and tender times we were able to share during our short time together. The other, the relationship with Sue had been on the decline, and the relationship was not what it had been at the beginning. The feeling was totally different when I was with Tanya.

So deep down inside I knew what I had to do. My problem was just how to do it. And now I realized that I only had about five or six weeks to figure something out. Unexpectedly, Tanya wanted to come to visit me in California during the last week of July. For one, the decision would not be a pleasant one. What should I do? I either had to call off my engagement to Sue or tell Tanya not to come.

During the high school years, I had another close and wise friend named Nancy. When she married Paul during our senior year, Paul asked me to be his best man. At that time, I had no idea what a best man was supposed to do except to be the best. After two kids and a lot of years of being married, Paul began to wander, which led to their marriage's demise. Over the few years, I stayed in touch with Nancy as often as I could. Some years later, she met James, and with their nuptial, they also had a son and a daughter. The reason I mention Nancy here should be apparent.

Because my Illinois sister, Dottie, knew how Tanya and I felt, I could call her, but I was afraid that her decision would be made from emotions and strong feelings for her close friend. Now, on the other hand, I could call my friend Nancy. I knew that she would be as neutral as she could be and also use her logic in her decision on what to tell me. Although I really already knew what I had to do, I wanted a second opinion. When I finally did call Nancy, she was anxious to hear about the trouble I had gotten myself into.

She listened intently as I told her about the entanglement and my deep feelings for the midwestern belle. After some thought, she did advise me to do what my heart was telling me to do. Now that was really good advice, because I didn't know for sure what language my heart was speaking. As a good friend would, she got to the point and told me that in order to be happy, she suggested that I really needed to call the engagement off and break up with the fiancée if I had the strong feelings as I described for Tanya.

That's what I was afraid of and dreaded, because I knew that was what I had to confront and do. The one thing that I did not ever want to do was to break someone's heart. I may have done so as a teenager, but didn't know it. But now that I was older and a little wiser, breaking a heart was even less fun and much more painful.

With my Navajo Indian buddy from Vietnam coming to visit me the first week of July and Tanya coming for a week the last week of July, I knew that I did not have very many weeks or days left to confront and deal with the tidal wave that was going to destroy a lot. This confrontation was one of the hardest and most uncomfortable things I'd ever had to attempt. I had no idea how to do it or how to deal with the storm that I knew would follow.

Sue could tell during the few hours that I spent with her that something was wrong. She knew that I was not the loving and caring person that I had been, and she insisted that I tell her what was going on. When it was finally time for me to tell her and leave, she accompanied me to the door and we continued talking outside. Reaching way down in the depths, I was able to pull out some courage to relieve the painful agony that we were both experiencing. Telling her that I couldn't be engaged to her and the reason why actually broke both our hearts. I had to admit to Sue that I didn't care enough to be able to make a permanent, long-range comment and didn't love her as I should. Both of our hearts were broken, mine because I do not take pleasure in hurting someone.

A long period of tears and attempts and promises to change of course came too late—about two years too late. On the drive home, I couldn't help but think of the terrible tsunami that I'd caused, but I knew that it had to be done in order for both of us to have an opportunity to either stay in the same state that we were in or choose to move on and start anew.

The following couple of weeks were difficult as I attempted to return to a normal life doing what I need to do. However, one late afternoon as I was working on my '64 Corvette, my phone rang while I was laying on my creeper. After cleaning my hands, I returned the call and found out that Sue wanted me to return everything that she had bought for me during the two years of our relationship.

I asked her, "How am I supposed to know which things you bought?" After a month, guys usually don't remember what was purchased.

I agreed to allow her to come over to my house and pick out the items that she recalled. On the day of agreement, she was accompanied by her parents, whom she still lived with. While her mom walked back and forth across the backyard lawn, we were in the master bedroom sorting through the shirts, pants, and a die-cast Corvette models. When I suggested to her that I would pay her for the items so that she would not have them lying around or have to donate them, she said that she did not want me to have anything that she had bought for me. As she sorted through the clothes, I retrieved her a box and bag to put the items in. As we exited the back door, her mother was still patrolling across the lawn as if she were just looking at things. There was really nothing to look at. The tsunami had arrived and caused the damage. As they backed out of the driveway, I could feel a warming and comforting it's-finally-finished feeling as it began to engulf my senses.

Chapter 13

The following week was spent getting ready for my Vietnam bud to arrive and talking to close friends. When Richard arrived, he did so by rail. He did not like to fly, except to come home from the battlegrounds that we shared. A couple of days passed while I gave him a chance to adjust to the California weather. On the third day, we headed for the hills and ended up in Yosemite National Park. I knew then that he was an artist who painted murals. On a road trip along I-40—the old, original Route 66—through Gallup, New Mexico, a person is able to enjoy his artistic works that are on the side of the building. As a matter of fact, he improved my book covers.

While in Yosemite National Park, we took pictures of about everything. Richard was busy taking photos of scenery, including the Half Dome, the gorgeous waterfalls, the winding trails, and the unusual shapes of the trees. I hoped that he would be able to use some of the pictures he took.

When we returned to the valley, we spent the remaining days visiting, sharing memories, and touring around the time. I was sadden to see the day come when my buddy had to return to his ground in New Mexico. Prior to his departure at the local train station, we bid one another a farewell. Even today, we stay in touch with each other.

Richard and I are both members of the 5/7 Cavalry

Association. Being members, we are able to share the info and other related issues that are of interest. This will allow us to catch up on a lot of other information during the cavalry reunions. Although Richard's leaving was somewhat sad, I became very excited and hoped that the next couple of days would pass quickly. The two days would give me a little time to plan the events for the visit of my next guest. And what a visit it would be.

The arrival and weeklong visit was very highly anticipated by me, and all of my neighbors were anxious to meet Tanya. The anticipated day finally arrived, and I was making a special trip to the airport. I waited with excitement for the arrival and landing of her flight. During the first week of August 1994, wouldn't you know on this special anticipated day, her flight would be arriving later than it was scheduled. The ten or fifteen minutes seemed to be more like about three or four hours. After waiting for what felt like half of a day, the intercom finally announced the arrival of flight 007 at gate seven.

I'm sure that my blood pressure was elevated to the outer limits, because my heart began to increase its rate of beats per minute, and for some unknown reason, the temperature inside of the terminal also seemed to be somewhat hotter than it had been when I first came in. The long wait and the excitement of her actually coming out to California to visit almost pushed my respiratory system over the limit. It didn't seem like another hour after the aircraft parked at gate seven before I saw her walking down the long corridor that connected the ticket terminal to the gate.

To see this woman whom I'd just met in May and knew I'd fallen in love with walking the hundreds of steps through the long corridor sent a chill down my back and interrupted the heat that was generated when my heart rate increased earlier.

If the TSA barriers would not have been in place to block and control the flow, I would have run at least a half of the way down the long corridor to meet her. When she finally walked past the barriers and we met again, it was like seeing someone I had known for years. She seemed to have a happy glow about her as we shared hugs and long kisses. There was a feeling that we were finally together again and how the fifteen hundred or so miles could not keep us apart.

After most of the other passengers had walked around the embracing couple standing in the path of everyone, we decided to gather up her luggage and head for home. We had some catching up to do and couldn't wait to get started with the plans. Upon arriving at my home and the hot August temps being hotter than normal, we decided to get comfortable and relax. I gave her the grand tour of my modest mansion and offered her something to drink. At this moment I can't recall if the offer was for water, beer, wine, or a soda, because I was like a child who had just received a long-awaited toy. The kind of drink didn't really matter much.

After a quick cool down, we both seemed to be thinking the same thing. That was to see if what we experienced in Illinois could be duplicated in the August heat of Fresno. After an hour and a good shower, we knew that there was no difference even though we'd been separated by the miles. She preferred to cook us dinner rather than going out to eat, so the first evening together we went to the store and purchased the few items that she would need to prepare our first special meal together.

It was probably because of the playing and frolicking that occurred during the preparation of the ingredients, but before the actual cooking of our long-awaited meal, we had to check the master bedroom to see if the temperatures had remained the same since we'd been there just their a hour or so earlier. After finding out that all was well, we returned to the kitchen an hour later to cook our dinner. Because Tanya is an excellent cook, I knew the food would roll over my curious taste buds and dance down my throat. As the delicious food would land and come to rest in my food tank, I would be receiving nourishment and energy for later in the evening. When the delicious meal had been devoured and the small amount of leftovers put in the fridge, we both joined forces to wash the dishes in order to speed the process up so that we could spend some time relaxing.

The following day was going to be long and busy. While we watched something on TV, it seemed that our hands were made to belong on each other's bodies. With the second morning rapidly approaching, we both felt it necessary to go to bed and get just enough rest to get us through at least a part of the next day. Our first night together in my bed was almost as exhausting as our last night in Illinois before I had to return to California. The clock must have been striking the hours without us knowing, because the time flew by.

Somewhere around three o'clock in the morning, we were both exhausted and collapsed while holding on to each other so as to ensure neither would get away. We overslept about an hour but were able to get up at about seven o'clock. As we began to get ourselves ready for the day, plans were made to go out for breakfast as we faced the warm sun. As I finished shaving and getting ready, she came into the bathroom I was using, and our hands once again began to explore the shapes and curves of our bodies as we pulled them closer to each other to feel the smoothness and warmth as they blended together and began to entwine.

During the summertime in the San Joaquin Valley. the days are very long and very warm. That was a very good thing for beginning our first true day together. Somehow, we finally made our first stop at a breakfast restaurant. After eating, our first day was going to be spent at Sequoia National Park and Kings Canyon National Park to meet the mighty giant redwoods and enjoy the beautiful sites and fresh air of the Sierra Nevada Mountains. And to do all this in a classic Corvette with a person who shared the same love and interest as I did, well, I couldn't ask for much more.

To reach our destinations, we traveled east on Highway 180 into the mountain area. Once we arrived at the parks, the left fork of the Y led us into Sequoia National Park first. When we were finished taking pictures and enjoying the breathtaking sights, we continued into Kings Canyon National Park to meet the mighty generals. For those who may be unfamiliar with the giant redwoods of California, the huge thousand-year-old giants had been named after some of the greatest generals of America's military might. The General Sherman and General Grant seem to greet the thousands of visitors from around the world every year as they continue to stand tall and strong.

As we completed our tour of the beautiful mountains and the parks, we continued our journey, returning to the Valley by leaving the mountains on Highway 198 (instead of Highway 180) and driving through Tulare County and Visalia where we rejoined with Highway 99. Returning to Fresno, we stopped south of town for a potty and refreshment break. After we rested for a short time, and being anxious to get back to my house, we got into the car, settled in, and guess what—my mechanical pride and joy would not start. It was still on a break. Being so embarrassed that I didn't know what to do, we just had to wait for the starter to cool off.

The car had pulled this type of stunt before. When I was able to again start it, we were on our way home. As we entered the house, we both began pulling off our outerwear in order to begin a cool down from the high temps and frustration from the car stalling. As the coolness delivered by the evaporated cooler began to surround us and cool us down while we sat on the living room couch, I took a nearby towel and began wiping the moisture from Tanya's glistening curves. She grabbed a second nearby face towel and started reciprocating my movements. The mutual massaging caused the flame to be sparked again. An hour later, the flame began to dim, and after a short rest period, we were in the kitchen warming up our leftovers. When the day ended, we could be found on the couch wrapped in each other's arms and our heads bobbing while we tried to stay awake.

The third day began the same as the second when we were a little late getting up. This day would take us north about ninety or so miles to meet some of my family and friends. Who would be more important to introduce her to but my mom and my second stepdad? (If you recall, my dad passed away in 1972 while I was attending Fresno State.) I knew that my mom would love and approve of God's choice for me given that the first two choices I made on my own ended up in disasters.

Since my second stepdad, Johnny, was a very judgmental person, I knew that his opinion would not sway me or change my mind. After a few hours of visiting with my mom, we left to visit my best friend, Nancy. Our visit with James and Nancy went well but didn't last very long because of a prior commitment that they had.

On our way back to Fresno, we both agreed on plans for the next couple of days but wanted to reserve a day just for us. Arriving back home on the third day, we had another long repeat of the prior evening—what a way to live.

The fourth day after our recreational events took us to

the central coast of California to the towns of Morro Bay and Cayucos. Both of these small towns are nestled on the shore of the great Pacific Ocean and have seals (not the navy kind) around the piers and rocks. The breezes blow gently through a person's hair as the white-capped waves rush upon the smooth, sandy beaches to meet the visiting people. As the wind blows across the beaches, one can see the white-and-gray seagulls floating on the wind currents, waiting for someone to have sympathy on them and fling some food their way.

The infamous California surfers can be seen paddling out to deeper waters on their surfboards in hopes of catching the big wave. For some reason, there are always those who want to walk on the sandy beach and look for shells and ocean weeds while their dogs and kids explore the areas a distance from the parents. There are many things that a person can enjoy when visiting the central coast cities of California. I was somewhat surprised to learn that Tanya had never seen the beauty and unusualness of the central coast.

She seemed to be speechless as she sat and opened her spirit and soul and allowed the awesomeness of her surroundings to just flow into her and captivate her senses. This area of beaches quickly became her favorite place to be.

After eating fresh seafood favorites and visiting with my younger brother (number eight of eight) and an uncle and aunt, we had completed a long, enjoyable day. But it was the bewitching hour and time to make the three-hour drive back to the smog and heat of the San Joaquin Valley. The long drive that was ahead of us offered an opportunity for us to share feelings and stories that either caused or helped each other to be in the place that we were currently in.

During my past talks with my Dottie, prior to me actually meeting Tanya, I was told about her cause and what had happened in her life. As we talked, I recalled how honest and open she was when we would talk for hours on the phone before we met. So I took the opportunity to ask her about her life and many situations.

I was sadden to learn that this wonderful and giving woman had been a severe victim of domestic violence. For seven and almost eight years, she had suffered and somehow tolerated the abuse and mistreatment. Her ex-spouse even stalked her and was trying to get her to come back to him. He was, and still is, the biggest jerk who has given up what could be the most important and generous person that he could ever know. Well, you can get the idea of what I think and feel about this lowlife.

When she finished telling me about her horrifying experiences while she tolerated this ordeal, I was almost left speechless (which is very difficult for me). Because I have PTSD, it was very difficult for me to hold down the anger and frustration that I was feeling. I told her that I felt that no human should ever treat another like that. She continued to describe living in a converted garage while she worked two and sometimes three jobs in order to pay rent and other expenses. She found out that while she was at work (mainly to avoid his abuse), her ex would be out partying and hanging out at the local bar and neighborhood establishments. (You have to know that I am paraphrasing and using reader-appropriate terminology.)

So while she was working, the ex was out spending her earnings as a big spender. She is not sure how she endured the physical and emotional abuse for the number of years that she did. Somehow, after seven-plus years, she finally realized that the situation was not going to improve, because it kept getting worse. The escalation of the substance abuse trickled down on her in the form of severe, out-of-control abuse. It became so frequent that she came to the conclusion that she had to either leave and get out of the terrible cycle or stay and be beaten down to the final point of death.

Just so you know, there will be more detailed information on how her exit occurred and how and who helped pull her to safety and out of the hell situation. The occurrences after she left and how her ex reacted and responded will be intriguing and may also give an insight for others who are in or have experienced the same infliction by another.

My book *The Children of the Wrath* will expose it, so watch for it. Because I am a former law-enforcement officer and have been an investigator for the State of California, I found what she was telling me almost too far-fetched to be believable. So after the three-hour drive and arriving at home, I had to call my Illinois sister, Dottie, to either get a confirmation or retraction from her on what I had just found out. After all, I had heard of abuse situations like this and seen movies that portrayed this behavior, but I had never been up close and personal to a victim who has overcome as Tanya.

The call to Dot was confirming of the events that had just been described, and in addition, she made me aware of the rest of the story, so I could make a clearer and more informed decision our future together if that would be the fork in the road that we would choose when the proper time came. With the information that I had received, I did not change my mind or feelings at all, so we spent the last two days together just hanging out and sharing the love for each other that had been sparked while on those simple picnics when we first met.

While lying in bed one morning, Tanya made a comment that I was her knight in shining armor that had rescued her and saved her. I really didn't know how to respond. However, I had been a Downey High School Knight in the sixties but never had shining armor. I could feel our love and deep, true feelings bonding together as we grew closer and shared all the feelings of love that we had. It's something that neither of us had ever experienced before and never with our exes.

And then like a blink of an eye, the morning had come for her to return to her home. This day would be one of the sad days—a day that I had not seen or felt since the day I had to leave my home to go to Vietnam. I know that Tanya felt the same way, because it took her much longer to get her bags packed and ready to leave than what is normal. When the last bag was closed and zipped up, we both laid across the bed and held each other tightly, both knowing that this would be the last time to share our caresses and love. So once again, we took advantage of the amount of time we had left to share the warmth and love that had grown between us.

Returning my new love to the air terminal to leave was another very difficult thing I had to do. To somewhat put an ease on the discomfort, feelings, and emotions, we both promised that we would call at least ten times a day and think of each other every minute of every day until we could be together again. In a few minutes, she disappeared down the same walkway connecting corridor in which I watched her arrive and walk to me a few days earlier.

Momentarily, the events of the past few days and the love that I would miss seemed to flash across my memory, and the realization found comfort in my mind that she was gone. Before I even opened the door to the car to return home, I knew that I was going to be alone. I almost heard a crack in my heart as it began to break from the emptiness. During the following ten or so weeks, many hours had been spent on calls between Illinois and California. We would call each other every free minute that we had each hour of each day.

For illustration of our phone rhythm, because she lived in the Central Standard Time Zone and I was living in the Pacific Standard Time Zone, there was a two-hour difference in our schedules, so we had to work out various times to call. She would begin work at eight in the morning, and it would be six in the morning for me. After an hour or so of anticipation, she would call me while I was getting ready for my day. When she would go on her first break from work at around ten in the morning, I would call because I was just getting ready to go to work at eight in the morning. Every opportunity or break I could get hold of, I would call her. This procedure continued every day and every hour. In the evening hour and until twelve midnight PST, we talked and took advantage of every minute that we were awake. Almost all of my friends and a few of the contractors who were referring me to work began telling me that it would be much cheaper to marry the woman so their calls could be answered.

Day in and day out, this procedure continued. Because there was an empty hole in my heart now needing to be filled and I knew that she also had damage to her heart, we both began to interject the subject of "more permanency" in our newly formed relationship conversations. We knew this would heal our hearts and close the holes.

Tanya mentioned a couple of times that she would be willing to move into the house with me to see how the relationship would develop. You have to understand that I had five sisters, and during this long-distance courtship, my mom was a vibrant, spunky eighty-seven years old and had told me many times that I wasn't too big or too old to have a belt placed swiftly across my hindquarters.

You have to remember that my mom was undercover tough. She survived the Midwest dust bowl storms with three girls and almost no food and no facilities. So you can only imagine her having a strong will and having very strong spiritual beliefs. I know that not only would she not be in favor of Tanya's proposal, but my mom would have reached for a belt or strap to change my mind. However, to avoid an old country lashing, I had to explain why her moving in with me would probably not be the best idea for being together.

As the days crept by, we both knew that our injured hearts wouldn't survive forever in the condition they were in. I had made plan to travel to Illinois for Thanksgiving, which just so happened to be a crucial, life-saving trip for us. In order to make the trip, which wouldn't be free, I had to work on some weekends to earn enough extra money for travel expenses. Because Richard had come to visit in July and then Tanya's visit was the first week of August, my reserve funds seemed to have left home and never to return.

One weekend I was in Modesto, the American Graffiti town, doing some repairs for long-time acquaintances. While at the old Lumberjack Building Supplies to purchase materials, I used a pay phone to call Tanya. Again, the subject of being together came up for discussion, not realizing that some pressure was applied so I could make a decision. During the last week of August 1994, and after some jittery and vocal stammering on my part, the sweet, understanding voice on the other end asked me, "Well, what should I do?"

I knew at that moment I was placed in a position to make a choice to, either live with and tolerate my injured and damaged heart or choose to have the acquired medicine for its proper healing. Although I had only known this woman for four months, I knew that she was to be my soul mate, and the time had come for a permanent decision if one was to be arrived at.

During the conversation, I finally decided to commit or not to commit. As my mind became confused by the sudden rush of various thoughts and of the unknown—I'd only known Tanya for four months, and I'd already had two failed marriages—I wondered if four months would be enough time to assure the third marriage would be a forever union. I do know that nothing is guaranteed or assured in life, and my heart needed to heal, so what the heck.

I responded to her question, finally breaking the silence that had engulfed the phone line while she waited for an answer one way or the other. So, I took the leap of faith and asked her for her hand and body in marriage. She must have been waiting for the question, because she didn't have to think about an answer very long. After she quickly accepted the long-awaited proposal, the glorious date was set for while I was going to be there for the Thanksgiving holiday.

Now, here is the math problem for you. I called Tanya from Modesto on October 15, 1994, and we were going to recite the happy nuptials that year after November 20 and before November 28. Keep in mind that Thanksgiving Day would be on November 24, and my birthday that year was on Friday, November 25. What would be the best date to have the ceremony performed? How many days did she have to make plans, choose the invitation design, and locate a church and minister? There wasn't enough time to put all the things together. Somehow, she planned and organized everything in four months from the time we met and about five weeks after I proposed to her.

I admit, it would be very difficult for anyone, but not this superwoman. I have to give credit to a woman who can complete a puzzle such as this in a very short time. I doubt if a man could do the same. She was able to accomplish all of these difficulties and still work her eight-hour shift at her job in about thirty-nine days. The ceremony wasn't going to be elaborate, just something simple and easy.

Chapter 14

On Friday, after a large Turkey Day, we both sat down for the typical counseling session with the pastor who had agreed to perform our ceremony. Due to the short notice, Associate Pastor Stover was a retired military chaplain who found it necessary to still cover all the bases of commitment, though we both had heard the responsibilities twice before.

After he spent about thirty minutes explaining to each of us our responsibilities and proper behavior toward the other person, he described to me the backdraft and reaction that could occur with Tanya as a result of the domestic violence that she had experienced. These were: sleepless nights, being afraid of the dark and shadows, and a fear that her ex would follow us to California, to name only a few. These results we could deal with as each reaction would arise. We both experience the PTSD symptoms, which has resulted from our traumas. We both felt at the time, and still believe today, that we were brought together by God for a purpose, which was unknown to us at the time.

The strength and understanding by each of us to face any difficulty that may arise in our relationship due to her trauma and the violence she was able to tolerate would be dealt with and overcome by both of us.

This meeting with Associate Pastor Stover was a blessing

and gift. The wedding plans were to come together on the following day. Early on that blessed Saturday morning, my sister Dottie and Tanya gathered their clothes and women's essentials and left to get prepared at the church. Jon and I hung out at their house until it was time for us to get ready for our arrival. Some minor touch-up decorating was done on the room in their house where the reception was going to be held.

Once at the church, my nerves began to rock and roll as Jon calmly escorted me through the double doors and walked me to the groom touch-up room. As the magic time grew closer, I began trying to wear the room's carpet out as I paced back and forth. It seemed like a day later we were finally summoned into the church's sanctuary to be placed in our areas and prepare for my lovely bride's walk down the bridal path.

Before my bride's leisure stroll down the magic path, Jon and I turned on the four movie cameras that we had set up and aimed so that the entire ceremony would be covered, and we would have proof of the happenings. About one minute after the four cameras were turned on, the large doors to the sanctuary were flung open, and I watched as the loveliest bride was holding on to the arm of her dad as they made their way down to the front. For the two previous marriages that she was involved in, her dad wasn't present or involved. So her dad being involved and being able to walk her down the aisle was a dream come true for her.

As they got closer to the front, I could clearly see the big smile on her anxious face and the look of "she's yours" on her dad's face. But little did she know, my blood pressure must have tripled and my heart was beating to try and keep up with the increase in blood pressure. This was it. Unlike almost all weddings around the world, our wedding ceremony was smooth and came off without any funny video scenes.

Etta James sang in one of her songs about the feeling and the love that we were experiencing. My dreams had finally come true, and my long search for true love was over. As our wedding pictures were being taken, for some unknown reason, I recalled the talk that each of us received from Dottie about treating each other good. She had to add that if one hurt the other, she would track us down. She has not had to put on her tracking boots yet.

After the ceremony and picture posing, everyone followed their noses and found where the food was. Tanya changed out of her mom's wedding dress and slipped into something more comfortable. After the speeches, toast, and cake cutting, we let everyone know that it was finished, and most of the guests left. Then we were off to the surprise location for our first night of having the popular titles of Mr. and Mrs. We arrived at a large, two-story house on the outskirts of town. Being a former peace officer and being unfamiliar with the area the house was in, I had to visually scan the yard, bushes, and house itself. PTSD also will make a person paranoid of the unfamiliar.

We were greeted at the front door by two beautiful German dogs and their female master. The master welcomed us to the house and explained the house rules. Slow as I am on some things, I did surmise that this was a bed-and-breakfast facility. We chatted with the owner and hostess for a while to settle her suspicions, as well as our own. The German shepherds must have felt comfortable with us, because they lay relaxing near our feet.

The woman showed us to the room that we would be staying in for the night. We brought our own wine and snacks, because like when we first met, we were planning on a very long and exhausting night.

As we slipped into the whirlpool bath to unwind from the tension and activities of the day, we began sipping our favorite wine to assist with the relaxation. About half of the bottle and forty-five minutes later, we were beginning to resemble the wrinkles of a California raisin, so thought we had better get the long night started. As we lay across the large, comfortable bed we explored that which we had only been able to dream about while we were apart.

A thunderstorm had sneaked its way above us and began with a rolling thunder sound and then the crackling of the lightning. Does anyone actually think that a little thunder noise was going to interrupt the plans that we waited months to experience again? You've got to be kidding. While the music of the thunder played us its tune, I gave my new wife a thorough rubdown and massage. I guess it was the music of the outside activities that put her to sleep. I was struggling to keep my eyes open and finally thought, *Heck with it,* as the suffocating weight of the dark night began to rest upon my shoulders and push me down into the soft bed.

Needless to say, our plans for the first night as husband and wife must have been overcome by the harmony of the thunder and lightning as they danced out of the room, leaving us fast asleep. We both were awakened by the silence of the next morning and found ourselves in quite an unusual position. Because our hopes of the night danced to the music and out of the room, we both felt that not all was lost. About an hour later, we were both in the morning shower making sure we were both lathered up and cleaned.

Guess who met us as we came downstairs for our breakfast. The twin shepherds were dusting the floor with their tails and prancing in place in anticipation of our steps arriving on the floor. After our welcome, we sat at the table and enjoyed our delicious mixture of fruit and muffins while visiting with our gracious hostess.

After finishing our bounty, it was time to say farewell to our new friends and meet my new mother-in-law for church services. While in church and then on to a lunch, I could tell that my new wife's mom was glad and proud of her daughter. After many long years of suffering through a separation and confusing relationship of being kicked out of the house at sixteen, Tanya and her mother had made amends and forgiven each other.

After leaving her mom's, we returned to the reception house and began gathering our belongings and getting ready to pack up for the next day. This was a slow and unsure process due to a new marriage, a new life together, and a new state for her. We moved as if in slow motion, because the next day we would be leaving our most dear friends who had helped both of us and brought us together.

This would be one of the most difficult things for us as we began our life as one. We had our last dinner together with Jon and Dottie that night and ended watching a movie and talking. The next morning, which was a Monday, we loaded up Tanya's car, and after a light breakfast, we drove to the car wash and cleaned the car. To destroy some time while we waited for her credit union to open, we stopped by to visit her mom and then headed over to see her dad. After a stop at the credit union, she was ready to be whisked away. After the business was completed, we were officially on the road toward California.

Our third night of marriage was spent in Oklahoma City, where we stopped for the night. After a delightful Oklahoma meal, we spent the rest of the evening and late into the night sharing our feelings and enjoying what we had waited all day for after tempting each other. The next morning after breakfast, we were headed south on I-40 again.

The road between our stops seemed to be long and boring

most of the time. There was only one way that we could come up with to replace the boredom while we drove. It sure kept us happy and alert. About four o'clock on Tuesday evening, we decided to stop a little earlier to rest in Albuquerque.

I noticed that there was a light coating of snow on the ground. Neither of us really thought about the fact that where there is snow, there is cold. When we stopped and stepped out of the car to obtain a motel room, we were slapped in the face with the freezing chill. After a hot dinner, we settled in our room for another enjoyable night.

After the day of teasing as we traveled, we did need to settle in with each other. The next leg of our journey was across the vast desert of New Mexico and on to the long stretch and openness of the Arizona badlands.

Once we crossed through the state of my birth (you may recall the twelve-pound turkey that my mom gave birth to earlier in the writing), we found our next stopping place for the night in a town in Southern California called Needles, which is the first town in California on I-40. After leaving the desert and badlands of Arizona, Needles would be the last town that we would be stopping in for the night before arriving at my home (soon to be our home). The small town is a desert town, and when the wind blows across the land, so does the dust and dirt.

The next day was Thursday, and we were anxious to get to our home. After breakfast, we drove the long distance, only stopping for fuel and some food. We arrived at our playhouse at about nine o'clock that night and only wanted to see the bedroom. But as we entered through the back door, we found a Welcome Home sign, a bottle of wine, a few various colored balloons, and a beautiful bouquet of flowers, all left by my neighbors next door to welcome Tanya home and to the neighborhood.

Due to the late hour that evening, we chose to thank them the next morning instead of at the moment of surprise. Needless to say, the comfort of the bed was very welcomed by the two weary travelers. Being too tired to entertain, as we laid our heads down, we were able to welcome the morning light with the melting heat from our entwined and slippery bodies.

The beginning of this new marriage and relationship has brought both of us the love, security, and peace that we had both been searching for during the past years. None of our former mates understood or cared enough to really know us or what our concerns or interests were. Because we both live with PTSD on a daily basis, we have experienced the same type of trauma.

In future writing, you will be able to read about Tanya's plights and how she dealt with and overcame her lasting trauma, as I have mind. As our life together has unfolded and been welded together as one, we have experienced the profound joy of knowing that we had not known in the past. Much of our knowledge that has helped us grow and expand our lives has come from family stories that we have been able to listen to as we sprouted out of our youth.

These stories have helped us gain knowledge and strength that we have needed in order to become the persons we are today. Our family histories and bloodlines have given us the foundations to build on, which have, in turn, helped us to cope with and survive the many trials and tribulations that we have had to go through in order to get where we are today.

Just as our experiences have made our history from today, everything yesterday and before is our history. This has been strongly influenced by, you guessed it, our families' histories and the stories that have been handed down generation after generation. After reading the timeline of my life experiences and gaining knowledge of my ancestors' plights as they walked their timeline of life, hopefully you will be able to draw a conclusion and better understanding of how I was able to withstand the pressures and diversities while walking my own life timeline. From being an offspring of two emigrants from the dust bowl days and low-income farm laborers who had a limited education, I learned that hard work and perseverance would help me expand my knowledge and enable me to survive whatever situational task I was confronted with.

And where do you think these built-in genes came from in order to be able to do this? As most all people in the world, my own challenges, struggles, and experiences are a reflective result of my parents' own difficulties, which, in turn, were also of their parents. All of this, in a capsule, makes me, as well as all the people around me, wonder where we were yesterday, who we are today, and where we will go tomorrow.

We all must go and make our own histories, grow our own family trees, and tell the stories of the past. Just as my parents left the Midwest and traveled west in search of happiness and prosperity, it happened that Tanya left her life and all she had known to move west. I had to return to the Midwest to find mine. Isn't it funny how history can relate us to our beginning and our end?

Happy reading.